Needs Assessment

A Systematic Approach to Data Collection

Ananda Mitra

SAGAMORE
PUBLISHING

Publishers: Joseph J. Bannon and Peter L. Bannon
Director of Sales and Marketing: M. Douglas Sanders
Director of Development and Production: Susan M. Davis

ISBN print edition: 978-1-57167-575-0
ISBN ebook: 978-1-57167-619-1
LCCN:2011920967

Sagamore Publishing LLC
1807 N. Federal Dr.
Urbana, IL 61801
www.sagamorepub.com

This book is dedicated to those who have sought reliable data and conducted accurate data analysis to make important decisions about how they serve others.

Contents

Acknowledgments

I would like to this opportunity to express my thanks to my wife and son as they have patiently tolerated the erratic writing schedule that was required to complete this book. Without a doubt, this book would not have been possible without the support and encouragement of Professor Joseph Bannon, who has pioneered the idea of doing scientific research to assist in public policy planning with respect to leisure and recreation. His work has inspired me to continue to develop this area of research. In many ways, I am also indebted to the staff of nearly 100 recreation agencies with whom I have had the opportunity to work over the last couple of decades. I have learned from conducting studies for these agencies, and I have learned from the thousands of people I have had a chance to meet in nearly 700 focus groups over 20 years. All of their input helped me to write this book. Of course, this book would not have been possible without the support and encouragement of my family across the world, my colleagues at Wake Forest University, and a rich tapestry of friends. I am indebted to you all.

Preface

The idea of collecting citizen input before making decisions that would affect the lives of the citizens is fundamental to a democratic society where the people in power are supposed to serve the citizens who put them in charge. Furthermore, collecting this information becomes crucial when it is the citizens' money that would be spent by those in power. To conduct public planning without bringing the "public" into the process seems to miss the mark of sound planning for local governments. This book provides a road map for collecting citizen input that is reliably collected and honestly used. Consultants use a variety of ways to collect citizen input, and the methods vary in rigor and the quality of information produced. Unfortunately, much of what is touted as "citizen input" serves as "dog and pony" shows where the citizens get a feeling of being involved without any reliable and trustworthy data coming from "public meetings" and such events that are periodically held by consultants. This book provides a rigorous approach to collecting citizen input. As is the case in any scientific method, this book offers a treatment that can be conducted by anyone who is able to follow the directions in the book correctly. This makes the process repeatable and testable, both of which are critical to the scientific method. For the recreation practitioner, this book illustrates the best practices of collecting citizen data, and most importantly, allows the recreation professional to recognize unscientific attempts at citizen data collection and to be wary of information generated by less reliable methods.

Foreword

by
Dr. Joseph J. Bannon, Professor Emeritus
University of Illinois

I first became acquainted with Ananda Mitra in the early 1980s when he was a staff member at the University of Illinois Survey Research Laboratory. He was involved in developing needs assessments and community surveys, and I asked him to evaluate several questionnaires created by the Office of Recreation and Park Resources at the University of Illinois. I discovered that he was extremely well qualified in the area of needs assessment and understood survey research better than anyone I had ever dealt with.

As a result, he then became a colleague, and we worked together over the years to conduct over 100 needs assessments for park and recreation agencies throughout the country, evaluating and reporting on the recreation and leisure needs, desires, and future developments in numerous communities. Ananda understands the importance of eliciting supportable data and making it accessible to agencies in a reliable and user-friendly manner so they may more efficiently and effectively meet the needs of their constituents.

Assisting agencies in these vital needs assessments has become more important than ever in the current economic climate with its focus on leaner budgets and operating funds. All public agencies must critically analyze all expenditures, facilities built and maintained, and programs offered in a continued effort to better serve the public with a decreasing supply of discretionary cash.

Community health has become a high priority across the nation. Changing population demographics in the last decade have reflected the growing number of baby boomers reaching senior citizenship. This section of the population is growing at a rapid pace and is far more active and healthy in its retirement years than in generations past. This important constituent group will increasingly consider and in fact demand more opportunities to partake in active and healthy activities in their communities.

In this book, *Needs Assessment: A Systematic Approach to Data Collection*, Mitra explores important concepts in collecting citizen input and describes specific techniques and methods of accurate and relevant data collection. He underlines the necessity of using proper methodology to develop reliable questionnaires for adults and youth that will produce quantifiable and supportable data. He also outlines the importance of focus groups and how to conduct them in an effective way to provide citizens with sat-

ix

isfactory opportunities for input on all needs assessment topics in their communities.

There is a wealth of information in the Appendices covering sample questions for adults and youth, sample mailing pieces and emails, executive summaries, action plans, and presentation material. Mitra also discusses CompuRec, a program he personally developed, which allows agencies to take the information collected in the needs assessment and interpret the data to suite their communities' specific needs in ways never before possible. They can go far beyond the results reflected in the final report and extrapolate more detailed and specific information and apply it to their constituents' wants and needs.

Ananda Mitra has appeared at countless state and national conferences, giving presentations on systematic data collection and conducting needs assessments. Within these pages, you will discover much of the valuable insight he has gained while working with hundreds of board members, focus groups, and a wide variety of constituents about the importance of collecting reliable citizen input in needs assessments. *Needs Assessment: A Systematic Approach to Data Collection* does not just give direction about how to conduct surveys; it is a roadmap to creating action plans developed from the data collected to improve recreation and leisure facilities and opportunities for future generations.

1

Citizen Input as the Voice of the People

In a democratic system of governance, the most important element of decision making is the opinion of the citizen. In America, the entire governmental system is fundamentally based on the principles laid out in the Constitution, which puts power in the hands of the people who ultimately choose the people who run the government.

This same principle applies to every aspect of governance, where every citizen is offered the opportunity to provide a voice in the decision-making process. This principle was easier to apply when the citizenry was smaller; and it was possible for local governments to conduct meetings where every member of the community was present to voice an opinion and perhaps cast a vote when a decision was made. For instance, in Massachusetts, towns with fewer than 6,000 people are expected to make decisions through the open town meeting form of government, where every member of the town is expected to participate in a democratic process when a decision is being made by the local government (towns with more than 6,000 people in Massachusetts can make decisions using a representative town meeting form of government).

The voice of the citizen has played a critical role in the development of government and its services in the United States, and that same principle motivates the need for conducting citizen data collection with respect to parks and recreation management discussed in this book.

The primary focus of this book is the way in which recreation services are delivered to a constituency through a local government agency. This process of delivery is quite different from the form of recreation provided by private agencies. The difference in the way recreation delivery is managed by the public and private systems stems from a fundamental difference between the purposes of the entities. The private recreation provider, such as a health club, is in the business of making a profit by marketing its services to its most lucrative customer. The health club is interested in identifying a market segment that is most likely to pay for the privilege of using exercise equipment and would sell its services to that market. The club feels no obligation to market itself or to offer its services to a large population group as long as its target group is able to provide sufficient business. For example, the well-known national chain Gold's Gym first opened in 1965 in Venice Beach, California, and was targeted toward the body building sub-culture with Arnold Schwarzenegger as one of the early patrons of the first store. The focus on a target market with the intention of making a profit by providing a narrow set of services makes it simpler for private recreation providers to collect information from their market. The private provider is essentially interested in a "market" which will yield "customers" and "users," whereas the public recreation provider is interested in a "citizen," whose interests could be very diverse and who might never become a customer in the narrow sense of being a user of a recreation opportunity.

Every taxpayer is a part of the market served by a public recreation agency, and every taxpayer has a stake in the public agency, much like a stockholder would have an interest in a company. The public agency is also usually not interested in making a profit that will allow it to expand its services or add to its customer base. The profit motivation that drives the private corporation, and often determines the fate of a corporation, is far less urgent for a public agency. A public recreation provider is expected to offer a service to the community of taxpayers, as is evident in the mission statement of one of the largest public recreation providers in the United States, the Chicago Park District (CPD). It states, "Enhance the quality of life throughout Chicago by becoming a leading provider of recreation and leisure opportunities."

Although the mission also includes an assurance that the user will be satisfied by the opportunities offered by the CPD, the key to the mission is enhancing the quality of life throughout a massive urban area. The key to fulfilling such a mission is gaining an understanding of what the term "quality of life" means for the people in the service area, and then offering the people in the service area an opportunity to determine what services would indeed enhance their quality of life. This can only be done by returning to the basic democratic principle of allowing the citizen to have a voice, albeit one that is more detailed than the casting of a "yay" or "nay" vote, but actually returning to some form of the "town meeting" of the New England states where the citizen can actually elaborate on an issue before casting a vote. As such, the "vote" and "voice" do not become synonymous within the realm of recreation services. The vote can result after the citizen has had a chance to voice opinions about quality of life, but a vote alone is insufficient to gauge what the citizens want in terms of recreation services that enhance the quality of life.

The matter is specially complicated for public recreation providers as compared to other public agencies, such as a police or fire department, where the quality of life is somewhat simpler to define. For example, a police department would be interested in keeping neighborhoods safe. There is not much leeway or debate about the definition of the notion of good quality of life for the police department. Most taxpayers would want safe neighborhoods. The matter is more complicated with parks and recreation services because the quality of life could vary widely between different sectors of the population. The quality of life of young mothers with children would be enhanced with safe playgrounds, whereas the quality of life of a teenager would be enhanced with good video game parlors. Such variations in the expectations make it important to go beyond the vote when determining policy related to parks and recreation services.

The voice of the people, their opinion, their needs, their complaints, and their accolades need to be heard in order for the public recreation provider to serve the population that pays for the existence of the recreation agency. It is this focus on voice that makes it critical that parks and recreation agencies spend effort to collect input from citizens they serve, and the fundamental definition of citizen input rotates around the notion of voice, where the person who is being provided the service can become an agent of change in a democratic system. Indeed, without this voice, the system becomes autocratic where the recreation agency is the agent of change (or lack thereof) and the people being served become powerless in deciding the role of recreation in enhancing quality of life. Citizen input, by definition, thus becomes the material in a democratic system that offers people the power to define their destiny with respect to recreation and leisure.

Whose Voice?

The fundamental principle driving the collection of citizen input is embedded in a democratic principle that dictates that policy decisions are driven by feedback from the people who are affected by the policy. This approach to gathering citizen input is specially dependant on who, among the people, have the rights and abilities to voice themselves. Early democratic systems, such as those in ancient Greece and Rome, automatically excluded half the population—women—from participating in a democratic process because women had neither voice nor vote. That tradition of the classical period was continued in America until 1920, when the Nineteenth Amendment of the American Constitution allowed women the guaranteed right to vote. The democratic system is dependent on ensuring that all members of the system have an equal right to have a voice and a vote in the decision-making process. As a corollary to that proposition stands the abhorrence that democratic systems should have for special interest groups who might have clout to make changes that benefit the special interest group without bringing any improvements in the quality of life of others. It is also not unusual for special interest groups to set up systematic lobbying, even by placing their representative in decision-making positions, so that the special interests would be served better than the interests of the community at large.

There are many different ways in which the process of special interest service is guaranteed within the decision process for parks and recreation agencies. As any director of a recreation agency will attest, there often are people from special interest groups who are regular participants in the open meetings held by local governments. For instance, members of a special sports club could ensure that a large number of their patrons are present at all city council meetings where recreation-related matters are discussed. In an age of the Internet, where meetings agendas are often available on the World Wide Web (Web) it is not difficult to find out what decisions would be made at a future meeting. Special interest groups can ensure that their members are present in the audience, and could easily dominate the public commentary segment of the meeting by presenting the needs of their special group. Repeated presence at meetings, and a consistent request for services and facilities, could eventually sway elected officials who might acquiesce to the demands of special groups, and commit public money to do things that might only be of benefit to the special group. Such moves run contrary to the basic purpose of a recreation agency, and such follies can be avoided by remaining true to the process of collecting citizen input.

The process of collecting citizen is designed to avoid the biases related to special interest groups. A scientifically reliable and properly executed citizen data collection effort would produce information that would represent the voice of the entire community without favoring a more vocal group over a silent group. This component of citizen input is especially important because the composition of the vocal and silent groups tend to change with time. Some people who might have been very loud about their needs at one time could become drowned out by a louder group. These changes are not necessarily reflective of the changes in the population, but arbitrary changes in the community. Citizen input must be sensitive to the systematic changes in the population and periodically collected data needs to reflect the consequence of the changes.

Voices that Change

The changes in the population characteristics lead to changes in the definition of the quality of life. In the first decade of the 21st century, America has witnessed increasing migration of people from Spanish-speaking countries, large numbers of baby boomers retiring from the workforce, and an increasing health awareness that leads to rethinking the idea of a good life.

Such changes have profound impact on recreation agencies as new forms of leisure activities are demanded by the population. Yet, not all the components of the new population may be vocal in their demands, and without the scope of providing input, some segments would simply be overlooked. This is why the process of collecting citizen input is not a single-shot, static process which is done once and then forgotten. A responsible public agency needs to be able to periodically collect citizen input and create a longitudinal database that allows the agency to track changes and see how well the agency is responding to changes. Citizen input takes on a temporal value as it allows for benchmarking with the same agency doing an internal comparison that spans over time. If many different agencies did the same thing, it could be possible to develop a national inventory of citizen input about recreation and leisure. Such a compendium could serve as the touchstone for benchmarking, and to see how citizen input changes over time. Needless to say, the way in which the input is collected is particularly important to ensure that the data can be compared to each other.

Voices that Matter

Having reliable citizen input data also serves an extremely important procedural purpose since many policy decisions could be adjusted by what the citizens might have to say. Public agencies have to make short- and long-term policy decisions that impact the quality of life of the people served by the agency. Some of the impact is most visible when parks and recreation agencies decide to do things. For example, the beautification of a neighborhood park becomes evident to many members of the population, just as ignoring the maintenance of parks can quickly attract complaints from the population. Yet, such responses are intimately tied to specific policy decisions made at every level of the management of a recreation agency. Citizen input can help to shape the decisions by providing a sense of direction for the recreation agency planners.

There are two major ways in which citizen input plays a role in the decision-making process. First, the voices of the citizens matter because the population must feel a sense of satisfaction with the service that they are paying for with their taxes. There could be many minor reasons for citizen dissatisfaction. For example, my research in nearly a hundred different communities in America show that citizens are mostly dissatisfied with the amount of information they receive about recreation opportunities offered by agencies, claiming that there is never sufficient information about recreation opportunities. Such input can be quickly translated into policy decisions where the agency explores innovative ways of reaching out to the population. This could lead to some changes in marketing policy like changing the emphasis to electronic communication from the traditional advertisement in local newspapers. However, that change in decision is not done arbitrarily, but is indeed based on data gathered through citizen input. Voices of the citizens can, and should, matter when such decisions are made.

Recreation agencies also have to make a second kind of long-term and high-impact decisions that could determine the path of the agency for many years. These decisions are often tied to a master planning process where an agency must create a strategic master plan to take into the future. Numerous decisions need to be made as a part of execution of the master plan after a plan has been developed and adopted. Many of the decisions can have a direct impact on the citizens that are served by the agency, and it is only fair that the citizen voices be given adequate weight when making decisions that would affect the citizens. It is therefore especially important to include an opportunity for the citizens to have a voice before a master plan is developed. Indeed, a plan that does not begin with the access to reliable citizen input is not a true master plan but only an internal document that the agency might have developed to chart its course. Such a document could be easy to produce but is essentially worthless since it does not include the voices of the citizens who are the most important component of the master planning process. It is also important to note that the voices that are used in the planning process must not only be those of the special interest groups, as pointed out earlier, but the master planning process must allow all segments of the citizens to weigh in on the planning process. Citizen input at the beginning of the planning phase can actually allow local governments to save resources since the citizens might be desiring things that could be quite different from the high-price items that the agency might have considered putting in. Thus, citizen voices should matter a lot in the planning process.

One of the key aspects of planning is communicating with the constituency that is served by a recreation agency. The process of providing recreation opportunities is closely tied to the way in which the people are informed about what is being offered. In nearly every one of about a hundred studies that I have run, one of the top three reasons why people do not participate in recreation programs is their lack of information about the recreation opportunities that are available. Yet, the directors of most of the hundred agencies would feel that they are doing all they can to market their services. Often, the disconnect lies in the fact that agencies have not paid adequate attention to the voices of the people who can provide some direction about the best way of reaching the constituency. The citizen voices matter because the citizens can let the agency know what works for the specific community. Incorporating that information in the marketing and promotional plans would allow the agencies to do the marketing in a targeted and efficient way, eventually leading to a more lean and financially responsible way of marketing its services. Listening to the citizens leads to an understanding of how to communicate with them.

In the end, the citizen voices matter because the citizens are the stake-holders for a public recreation agency. Although there are layers of leadership like a city council or a park board who are supposed to uphold the citizen voices, there could be gaps in the way in which such intermediary bodies work. Going directly to the citizen offers a way of collecting relevant information from the market as opposed to listening to a few people, like seven members of a park board, to make significant policy decisions. A scientifically valid process can produce data that can help inform different components of an agency's activities, some of which can lead to significant organizational change that would eventually benefit the community and the agency.

These benefits make the process of collecting citizen input a particularly important task for public agencies such as recreation providers. Yet, this process is often either ignored by the agencies or done in a way that is so fundamentally erroneous that the data proves to be more harmful that useful. This book lays out the best practices of collecting citizen input focusing on the specific scientific method that must be used and also focusing on the specific kinds of skills that are required to conduct a citizen data-collection process. The next chapter describes some of the key objectives that must be enumerated when collecting citizen input.

2

Key Objectives in Citizen Data Collection

Collecting data from citizens offers people in a community the opportunity to gain a voice in the process of policy making, where local governments must make choices between different kinds of recreation options. Allowing the people to gain a voice makes decision-making a democratic process where the decisions are based on the choices and tempered by what the people have to say as opposed to what administrators of local governments might decide on their own. At the same time, it places a responsibility on the decision makers to ensure that they fully appreciate whose voice is being considered in the decision-making process.

User vs. Non-user

Any community can be divided into two large broad groups—regular active users of public recreation and those who are relatively unresponsive to the opportunities offered by public recreation providers. Usually, the first group is called "users" and the latter the "non-users." There could many reasons (discussed later in this book) that make some users and others non-users, but the recreation agency seeking to gather input from citizens must make a decision about whose voice would be considered to be more critical. The usual tendency is to pay more attention to the voices of the users because they appear to be more involved with the activities of the agency. However, that is also akin to listening only to a single political party in a political campaign just because people with that political affiliation happen to be friendlier with the administrators. As a matter of fact, in making recreation decisions, it is necessary to attend to the voices of both users and non-users because both the categories are equally responsible for paying the taxes that support a recreation agency. In a typical study aimed at collecting citizen input, it is essential that both the users and non-users receive the same opportunity to have a voice. This could lead to a situation where the information is influenced by the fact that there will be people who will comment about issues that they are very familiar with, whereas there will also be people who might not even know that there is a public recreation agency that serves the community they live in.

A related issue with deciding on the segment of the community whose voice would become critical in the decision-making process is also deciding a well-accepted description of the "user." So far, the assumption is based on active use of public recreation. Therefore, it is possible to claim that those who come to a swimming pool all through summer can be considered users. By this definition, a person who would drive by a well-decorated park every day on the way to work, and for a moment enjoy the aesthetic quality of the park, is not a user, because there is no active use of a facility or program. However, anyone who feels that their morning commute to work is made a little more pleasant by the existence of well-maintained parks could also be considered a user of public recreation. It thus becomes difficult to come to a singular definition of the user, and any attempt to definitively describe the "user" could result in excluding a segment of the population from having a voice in public recreation decision-making process. It is usually wiser to implicitly assume that all taxpayers potentially served by a public recreation agency must be allowed the same opportunity to gain a voice.

Such a decision could also lead to a multiplicity of voices, where it could become very difficult for an agency to clearly identify major themes that would eventually shape the decision-making process. It is important to offer some structure to the way in which the data is collected from the large cross-section of people and the specific scope of the data-collection process. In some forms of interaction with citizens, it is possible to have an unstructured conversation where many people discuss a set of issues. In most such cases, it is usually a small number of people who are not representative of the community, and these people (often called special interest groups) would dominate an open-ended discussion to achieve their special and selfish outcome. This process is unrelated to the process of giving people voices as discussed so far. This is why it is incorrect to take the discussion from a public meeting or a focus group meeting and characterize those topics of the discussion as "citizen data." Indeed, the discussion outcomes of such small groups is completely unrelated to "data," and merely represents some of the issues that were discussed by a small handful of people who were interested in lobbying for their special interest.

On the other hand, the process of collecting data from citizens throws a much wider net where the data is obtained from a larger group, making it necessary to offer some structure to the way in which the data is collected and the specific kind of data that is collected. This structure is obtained from the purpose of doing the data collection. In its broadest form, the purpose of the data-collection effort is to listen to the voices of the people when making policy decisions related to recreation opportunities that would be used by the people. However, this broad purpose needs to be codified into specific areas of focus as demonstrated in the next section.

Describing Recreation

As pointed out by several researchers, the term "recreation" has a multitude of meanings (Bannon, et al., 1998). Over years of focus group research, and through conversations with numerous recreation professionals, I have seen that what is considered recreation varies by all the possible personal attributes like age, gender, race, ethnicity, income, educational level, and when the question is asked. For example, the 1990s in America witnessed a significant growth in the interest in rollerskating. Many teens in the 1990s would have considered rollerskating to be their primary form of recreation. However, a decade later, those same teens, now in their twenties, might consider hiking on weekends as recreation. There are numerous such examples that show that it is nearly impossible to pin down a specific definition or description that citizens might attach to recreation. In fact, it might even be futile, and somewhat counterproductive, to seek such a definition when listening to the voice of the people. It is often wiser to look for specific categories of activities that might fall into broad genres of recreation activities. When such a structure is imposed on the open-ended potential of recreation, it is also possible to collect coherent and usable data as opposed to a jumble of information that does not "hang together" in a reliable way. It is thus advisable to describe recreation around specific groups of similar recreation activities, and then labeling each group in a clear way. For instance, it is possible to collect information about hiking, walking, and bicycling and then club them under the rubric of "outdoor fitness" activities, or ask people about "outdoor fitness" and offer common examples of this category.

Citizens would then be able to voice their opinions with respect to any specific group of recreation activities without having to pick a specific set of individual activities to describe what recreation means, or the myriad of activities people could label as recreation. This makes it important to focus on recreation categories like "athletics" that could cover a range of activities from baseball to volleyball and people could voice their support for athletics knowing that the category would include the specific sport they are interested in. This basic information allows a recreation agency to develop a clear picture of the way in which the people think about recreation. The elaboration on the categories of recreation also leads to the point where it is possible to delve into a related category—what people feel is lacking with respect to recreation in a particular community as discussed in the next section.

Recreation Needs

The process of citizen data-collection points toward some of the key areas of recreation within a particular community allowing a recreation agency to develop a specific image of what a community might consider to be recreation. Sometimes the leadership of a recreation agency might already have a good sense of what the general categories of recreation are in a community, and the data-collection process helps to validate some of the information that the agency already has. The process of data collection also allows the leadership to validate the information about the needs of the community with respect to recreation. Very often, the staff of recreation agencies gets to hear about specific needs from the users of recreation facilities and programs. It is not unusual to hear about a dirty restroom, inadequate parking, or lack of practice fields from those who are regular users of the facilities. Such feedback offers a glimpse of a larger range of community needs, and the process of collecting citizen input offers a more elaborate and reliable method of collecting that information.

The idea of recreation needs often goes beyond the specific needs of special users groups. The community at large might have needs that are never clearly enunciated since some of the needs are broad-based and might not relate to specific users who show up at the Council meetings. For example, one of the key barriers to participation in public recreation activities is lack of information about the opportunities. People simply do not know what is going on and what is available. There is often a need for information, and ironically, those who need the information are often the ones who are least likely to show up at public meetings that are usually populated by the same faces who come back with the same complaints. Yet, the need for information is significant, and public recreation agencies should be addressing this matter. The process of citizen data collection can help to focus on such needs since citizen data collection is designed to reach a large cross-section of people who would often use the data-collection opportunity to voice their needs even if they have not been attending public meetings.

It is important to devote some attention to exploring public needs when designing the process of citizen data collection. The information that can be obtained from a correctly executed study can sometimes come as a surprise to the staff who might have felt that they had a good sense of the needs of the community. Unfortunately, the staff understanding of the needs are often shaped by the people that the staff get an opportunity to interact with—users. The citizen data-collection process opens up the process to a larger group who might have remained silent. There are numerous reasons why community groups remain quiet, and these reasons could range from feeling disenfranchised to a sense of apathy about government or general dislike for the public agencies. These factors point toward the general attitude of the population and these attitudes and opinions can have a significant impact on the way in which people interact with public agencies. As such, the process of collecting citizen input should also focus on the gathering information about the attitudes and opinions, as indicated in the next section.

What People Think

It is often the case that perceptions and attitudes shape what people might do. If, for example, people have one unsatisfactory experience with a single staff member, the user could develop a negative attitude toward the entire agency. A negative attitude toward some policies of local government can translate to negative perceptions about an entire agency. Attitudes and opinions about things that might not even relate to recreation could lead to specific perceptions about recreation agencies and their offerings. For example, if people feel that specific areas of a city are unsafe, then they might simply choose not to attend any recreation activities in that part of town.

It is also very difficult to gauge the general attitudes of a large group of people without using very specific methods of data collection. Speaking to a few users might elicit the strong positive (or negative) attitudes, but most people do not hold very strong opinions, but tend to fall in a "central" area of opinions. It is also a challenge to understand the opinions of such people, because they tend not to be vocal about their attitudes, and do not usually attend public meetings and city government hearings. The best way to gather reliable information from such people is by using valid methods of collecting citizen input where a large cross-section of people are able to voice themselves. The information can be used to develop a "map" of local attitudes where the range of opinions can vary from very strong positive to very strong negative, while offering an opportunity for the "neutral" and "centric" people to have a say as well.

The attitudinal information is especially important, because the way people think is influenced by a large range of factors; one of which could, for example, be lack of information. In many instances, people simply do not have an opinion because they have no basis to form an opinion. The attitude information, therefore, becomes a measurement of issues beyond simple likes and dislikes, but acts as a diagnostic tool to interpret other segments of information. Other information that is especially important relates to the behavior of a community. The opinions often shape what people do, and it is important to collect data about behavior when gathering citizen information.

What People Do

There is a large range of definitions of recreation that depend on numerous factors, but they often all have one commonality—most recreation involve some activities. Some of the activities—for example, those associated with athletics—are quite obvious, but others such as reading, watching a movie, or simply sitting in a park might not appear to be "activities" in the traditional sense of active recreation. Nevertheless, people obtain pleasure from recreation activities that tend to enhance the quality of life. It is useful to have a sense of these activities of the citizen when collecting citizen data. A detailed understanding of the activities can allow recreation providers to see how to deliver recreation to their constituency. This is a little different from the process of defining recreation discussed earlier, but focuses more on specific activities that people are engaged in at the time of collecting citizen data. Some of these activities might not fall within the traditional definition of "recreation," but could have a significant impact on the way people recreate.

For example, the way people gather information about the events and news about their community could have a big impact on the way people recreate and the way in which a recreation agency plans its functions. One of the key aspects of delivering recreation opportunities is ensuring that the community is aware of the opportunities. Awareness can be built by getting information out to the community in a way that fits in with the lifestyle of the community. There are many different ways of delivering information—from word of mouth to personalized e-mails—and the appropriate method depends on the way in which a people most often learns about thing around them. Some use the newspaper, others might depend on television to learn about recreation opportunities in the community, and a successful effort of citizen data collection should be able to gather data about the way in which people seek information about the community.

In a similar way, it is often useful for a recreation agency to get a sense of the range of recreation-related behavior of a community. As will be shown later in the book, some of the behaviors are very specific to a community, but impact the operation of a recreation agency. For instance, a community of people who put a great premium on behaviors related to healthy living could have different expectations from a recreation agency compared to a community where the behavior is more focused on arts and crafts activities. Some of the behaviors can be generalized to an entire community, whereas others could be far more focused and idiosyncratic to small groups of individuals. It is useful for the agency to learn of the possible range of things people do, and then connect the behavior to specific attributes of the people.

Who the People Are

Most community-level data-collection efforts—ranging from marketing surveys conducted by local businesses to national polling agencies collecting data related to political attitudes—often collect information about the people who respond. This information might not include identification data, but it certainly helps to create a profile of a person or community based on the basic attributes of the people who respond to a data-collection effort. This information is commonly called demographic data and typically includes information similar to what is included in a census of the population.

It is extremely important to collect demographic information when collecting information about the recreation-related issues in a community, because many of the related issues are connected with the demographic attributes of the people. For example, data from numerous studies would demonstrate that men and women have slightly different opinions about leisure activities just as people with different levels of income could have different ways on recreating. Such differences would not come into focus unless the data-collection effort pays attention to the demographic structure of the people who are speaking.

It is also important to note that specific questions about the demographic attributes must be included in the process of collecting citizen data because the specific recreation-related responses must be tied to demographic attributes. Most communities in America would have standard census data describing the nature of the community, but that data cannot be connected with recreation-related responses, making it especially critical that demographic questions be included in the data-collection effort. Some of the demographic issues could also be quite specific to the people in a community, where very specific personal attributes could have an impact on the behavior and opinions of the people. For example, when listening to the voices of people spread out over a large county, it is critical to understand the primary modes of transportation for the community, whereas that issue could be much less relevant in the case of people clustered in a densely populated urban area. Such specific issues mean that the standard census data is often not sufficient to provide a complete picture of the people whose voices are being heard, and the citizen data-collection effort must be geared toward collecting information about the people.

Customizing a Study

The different issues described in this chapter offer a general overview of the key aspects of collecting citizen information. What people think about recreation, how people recreate, what their future needs are, and who the people are, are all issues that can be considered to be critical information for most groups of people. However, specific communities could have very special situations where the voice of the people becomes an important aspect in making policy decisions. For instance, there might be a situation in which people must provide their say on decisions related to specific buildings or parcels of land. In a similar way, what people think about a specific facility could influence the way it is used or future facilities that are designed. The process of collecting citizen data with respect to recreation must pay attention to such specific issues to create a customized process that is true to the basic purpose of the project—collect reliable data from the citizens.

The above purpose is also dependent on the specific methods used to collect the information, and the next chapter examines the basic social scientific principles that guide the process of data collection.

3

Methods of Collecting Input

It is not uncommon to see recreation providers sending out Requests for Proposals (RFP) that solicit help in collecting citizen data, often in connection with a planning effort. In the many years of reviewing RFPs, I have seen two key ways in which the citizen data is sought. Some agencies would state that citizen data collection should be accomplished through public meetings where people would gather in a room and a qualified moderator of meetings would collect information by a process of discussion with the people. Other RFPs would clearly note that there needs to be a "survey" that would be sent to the citizens to collect information. In such cases, the RFP could call for a systematic analysis of the data that is obtained from the community.

Qualitative vs. Quantitative Methods

The two processes of data collection used in numerous RFPs point toward two different methodological approaches that have been common for a long period of time in social science research. The use of public meetings falls within the qualitative approach to data collection, whereas the collecting numerical data from a community is often called the quantitative approach.

The qualitative approach has many roots, amongst which the strongest connection is with the tradition of research in anthropology. Those scholars who were interested in cultural anthropology were interested in finding out how other cultures operate. Researchers such as Clifford Geertz were especially interested in understanding the specific characteristics of relationships and behavior among people of a different culture. These scholars suggested that such knowledge could be obtained by a close observation of the behavior of those in a different culture. The researcher would collect the information from the observation and then draw specific conclusions about the group of people. Naturally, the final results of such data-collection methods, also known as ethnographic methods, were dependent on many factors that might influence of the quality of the data. First, the findings could be influenced by the specific people who would be observed. For instance, if a researcher were interested in understanding a foreign culture, then the understanding would be dependent on the specific groups that would be observed. The fact that groups have differences amongst them, as in the case of those who are interested in athletics as opposed to those interested in the arts, the final outcome of the qualitative data-collection process is dependent on the groups who were actually observed. Secondly, the quality of the data is dependent on the skills of the specific researcher doing the observation. Those ethnographers who have a good "eye" and "ear" for the details of human and group behavior might find things that would be missed by other researchers.

The experience and training of the researcher become important factors in what is observed and how it is recorded and communicated. In qualitative research, the personal opinions and biases of the researcher become key components of the final data. Indeed, this was one of the primary criticisms of cultural anthropology, because often the researchers would hold biases about the cultures they would observe and designate a foreign culture as civilized or not based on the bias of the researcher. This is tantamount to saying that a specific recreation interest is unimportant because the researcher is uninterested in it. The qualitative method eventually produces data that is made up of detailed descriptions of groups and people, and the quality of the data is dependent on how well the researcher is able to use words to describe behaviors and attitudes.

The dependence on words is reduced considerably in the quantitative method of data collection, which has its roots in the tradition of social and psychological research that was popularized by European scholars like Lazarsfeld, who were interested in measuring human behavior and attitudes using systems that were similar to the work being done in the laboratories of natural sciences. The quantitative researcher would consider this brand of research to fall into the area of social science, where the approach to data was governed by a sense of objectivity using the *lingua pura* of science—numbers.

Social scientists suggested that it is possible, albeit with limitations, to quantify specific components of human behavior and attitudes. For instance, it is possible to measure how many times a person remembers going to a park within a specific period of time, just as it is possible to place a number on the strength of a belief, for example, about the level of safety in parks. The quantitative approach suggests that a sufficiently large number of measures, when collected in an unbiased manner, provides the numeric data to draw some conclusions about a large group of people. These conclusions are unfettered by the biases of the researcher and are based purely on the numbers that are obtained from the community. In such cases, there is little doubt, as long as the data collection has been done correctly, about the feelings of the community that is being observed.

Historically there has been a chasm between the two different approaches for data collection. The division between the two groups is philosophical as well as pragmatic. The qualitative researcher is often spawned from academic disciplines that would be categorized more as departments of humanities, where researchers and scholars are more interested in the in-depth exploration of human behavior and feelings. These scholars are convinced that human attitudes and behaviors are immensely complex phenomenon that need to be studied carefully and skillfully before it is possible to understand their intricacies. This observation must be conducted by trained researchers who are able to understand, interpret, and write about the details of the behavior and attitudes of people who are being observed. To such researchers, reducing human behavior and attitudes to mere numbers seems to oversimplify a complex process. The quantitative researcher would maintain that the numbers help to move away from the personal biases of the qualitative researcher whose data is often impossible to generalize because the data is inherently biased by the groups that were observed and the biases of the researcher.

The quantitative scholar is often driven by the need to develop reliable generalizations about a specific community where biases are kept to a minimum. The goal of quantitative research is to produce a snapshot of an entire community so policy decisions can be made without the lingering doubt that the data used as the basis of the decisions is not tainted by biased groups or biased researchers. Indeed, quantitative researchers would make the argument that once the data has been collected, it is possible to replicate the findings by repeating the same method. Such repeatability of the study shows the quantitative researcher that this method produces reliable data that can confidently be used for decision making.

Selecting a Method

The debate between those who propose the quantitative method and those who support the qualitative method has a significant amount of academic value. Different universities would focus on different research methods, and those completing advanced educational degrees at different institutions would emerge with specific methodological biases. There is a difference in the way that researchers are trained depending on the specific methodological bias adopted by the researcher, and often those trained in one approach might only be able to conduct research using the method that they have specialized in. This division in training also spills over into the pragmatic world of collecting citizen data.

Professional staff members at recreation agencies need to make choices about the ways in which citizen data is collected. This choice is also based on the way in which the professional staff is trained, and often this choice is elaborated in RFPs and plans of work adopted by agencies. Many agencies release RFPs that specifically state that a survey is necessary to collect citizen input. Some agencies would require several public meetings as a way of collecting citizen input. As noted, each of the methods has different kinds of biases associated with them, and recreation agencies often end up working with inadequate data because they make important policy decisions based on the methodology used to collect the data. It is therefore important to make methodological decisions very carefully.

It is also important to note that many of the issues related to receiving "bad" data are based precisely on the fact that research decisions are made by focusing too much on methodology without paying sufficient attention to the reason and purpose of the research. It is often the case that recreation agency leadership begins conversations by saying, "We want to conduct a survey," or "We want to hold public meetings." Such *a priori* statements display their methodological bias but fail to focus on the *most important* issue in such studies—the research question (i.e., the reason the study is being conducted).

The correct starting point is to enumerate the reasons the study is being done—determining the "why" question before moving to the method, or the "how" question.

It is important to always remember the fact that the process of collecting citizen input is indeed a research endeavor, and as such the process should follow the best practices of doing social science research. In those practices, the most important question is stating the purpose of the research, often in terms of a set of broad research questions, and then seeking the best method to answer the question. For example, if the research question is to understand the ways in which a specific public property like a neighborhood park should be developed, then it is a much more restricted research question than trying to understand how an entire master plan should be developed for a large metropolitan park system. The difference in the purpose of the research should determine the specific method. It is extremely dangerous to settle on a method before clarifying the reasons for doing the research.

Starting with a clearly defined research question provides a specificity to the process and also allows the agency staff to maintain control of the process; this is particularly important if the process is being conducted by an independent group of researchers. As described earlier, different researchers and consultants have different biases based on their training. The consultants often influence the agency to adopt the method that the consultant specializes in without being sensitive to the purpose of the study. It is important for agencies to avoid falling into this trap and to work with researchers who are able to guide the process in the correct manner to answer the research question as opposed to promoting a preferred method. Academic research groups like Management Learning Laboratories (www.m-l-l.org) emphasize that the purpose of the study needs to be correctly stated before settling on a methodology. Indeed, it might be the case that after considering the purpose of the study, it is necessary to use a research method that combines elements of both the qualitative and quantitative methods.

A combined method of data collection results when the process begins with the research question and not with a focus on a preferred method. Ideally, all research should begin with a specific set of questions that operationalizes the purpose of the research endeavor. In the case of organizations that provide recreation opportunities to a community, the questions can address a multitude of issues. For example, the agency could be interested in the future needs of the community, and the purpose of the research is to examine what the community might claim to be its general requirements. Such a question cannot be answered by simply conducting planning meetings during which architects come in and show flashy slides of possible plans and then seek the input of the people who attend the meeting. Such a process does not answer the research question at all, but actually imposes on the community the agenda of the architects hired by the agency.

Research questions are correctly approached by collecting data in a systematic manner where a standardized tool, like a questionnaire, is made available to a group who represents the community. The data collected from the group then becomes the foundation on which planners can build their plans, instead of the top-down approach that is adopted by most planning consultants. When answering a question like "What are the future needs of a community?", it is wise to rely on a quantitative approach to collecting the data. However, it is also important to note that there might be specific nuances within a community that a standardized questionnaire might not be able to capture very well. Communities are usually not identical to each other, and there are often sufficient differences between communities such that answering the same research question for different communities could require slightly different questionnaires. Questionnaires must reflect the differences among communities, and data collection must be sensitive to these differences.

In such situations, it is important to obtain ethnographic information that can be used to design the appropriate questionnaire. This is done using qualitative methods by utilizing focus group meetings and workshops where the researcher can spend time speaking to community members. These meetings, as discussed later in Chapter 4, are well-coordinated discussions and should not be the "dog and pony shows" put together by some planning consultants. The meetings have a clear purpose and protocol and follow a process that can be repeated with different groups. Often such meetings can allow the researchers to design the appropriate questionnaire that would be used for the numeric data collection.

Many research projects would combine the meetings and the questionnaire to obtain robust answers to the research questions and thus meet the purposes of the study. When recreation agencies choose to work with re-searchers who are trained in both the qualitative and quantitative approaches to research, the agency can hope to obtain the most reliable answer to their research questions; often, combining the methods can produce the most ef-fective data. Usually the separation between the methods is an artificial divide caused by the fact that some researchers are better at one method than the other, and planning consultants are usually not very good at either method. The unevenness in research expertise among the people who are responsible for conducting studies causes the selection of one method over another.

Starting with the research questions and then selecting the appropriate combination of methods rather than committing to one method and forcing the research questions to fit the pre-selected methodological approach will result in cultivating the most accurate data.

4

Talking to the Community

Most communities in America have similar concerns related to recreation and leisure and the process of collecting citizen input demonstrates these similarities. Having been involved with nearly a hundred studies across the country, I can safely say that the decade following the 2001 attack on New York saw an increase in the interest in family-based recreation across the USA. Such trends can be observed in the data collected from a sample of the population who have responded to a standardized questionnaire that asks about overall recreation-related behavior, attitudes and interests. Yet, there are sufficient differences between communities that it is incorrect to take a standardized questionnaire and use that across different communities, especially when the goal is to collect information about the specific group of people to help make decisions that would help plan the recreation opportunities for the group. In those situations it is important to move away from a "one-size-fits-all" model of questionnaire design to a process where the data collection instrument is indeed designed to accommodate the unique issues in a particular community.

These issues are ones that the local recreation provider might be aware of as a member of the community. For example, most directors of recreation agencies can quickly name the group of people who lobby for a specific activity or facility. Many communities would have people who attend all the public meetings offered by the recreation agency to speak about the same issue independent of the purpose of the meeting. These are the people who make it a point to let the elected officials and the staff of a recreation department know the specific demands of the interest group they might represent. As discussed earlier, their insistence actually makes the issue appear much more important that it might be. The effectiveness of these groups is proportional to the "volume" of their voice, and often they can say the same thing. Their volume might allow their narrow interests to be met at the cost of the interests of the community at large.

Yet, the pronouncements of these groups do serve the important purpose of pointing toward some of the local issues that should be considered in the creation of the questionnaire. The questionnaire offers the opportunity to acknowledge the fact that the issue has been brought up by some members of the community, and then the importance of the issue is measured by asking questions about the issue to a scientifically valid representation of the entire community. The data obtained from quantitative component of the study can help to demonstrate the importance, or lack thereof, of the issue that might have dominated numerous public meetings. Furthermore, there could be many different issues that are specific to different components of the population served by a recreation agency, and all the different issues need to be placed on the proverbial table so that they have a chance of being considered carefully as the questionnaire is designed. Bringing forth the different issues is accomplished by the process of conducting focus group meetings.

Elements of the Focus Group Meeting

Focus group discussions have been used in a variety of settings. For example, focus groups have been used to collect information for market research, college and school student perspectives in academic settings, with managers and teachers, and community groups such as parents and community members. Focus group meetings with such populations have been used to gather qualitative information about specific issues from unique groups of people. A large portion of focus group meetings are used to collect data from a specific group of people; the researchers might stop with the focus groups and not extend the data-collection process to the quantitative stage.

However, some researchers have proposed the use of focus groups in the process of questionnaire construction. They point out five primary uses of focus groups in questionnaire construction. These include: (a) development of terms and phrases that the community uses in talking about services, (b) development of answer categories that reflect real-world perceptions, (c) development of meaningful response categories, (d) selection of a set of rating dimensions, and (e) generation of a battery of descriptive statements that become the basis of segmentation analysis. Each one of these elements is an important aspect of the way in which the focus groups are conducted in the case of recreation-related research.

Communities have a special language that they use within the community that distinguishes a specific group of people from others. This does not refer to language as in English or Spanish, for example, but to the actual terms and names that are specific to the community. The focus group meetings elaborate on such specific issues that help to produce a questionnaire that is more relevant and meaningful to the community. The issue of relevance continues with the other aspects of questionnaire design, where the focus group meetings allow the researcher to understand what specific responses would be suitable for the specific population. For example, if one of the goals of the study is to understand the different ways in which a recreation agency could be financed, then the focus group meetings help to develop the different options that the respondent can choose from. These options are often very specific to the community and can only be discovered through the focus group process. Eventually, the focus group meetings offer a great degree of in-depth information that helps to create a questionnaire that the respondents would recognize to be specific to the community, making it more relevant and yielding a higher response rate. Administration of focus groups helps in designing a questionnaire that best fits the community while retaining an overall generic structure.

There are usually two direct ways in which focus groups help to make a questionnaire specific to a community. First, focus groups help to obtain a community-specific input about the various recreation issues that are of importance to the community, and secondly, focus groups help to design a final instrument that is appropriate for the specific leisure program being studied. A third indirect utility of the focus group lies in the intrinsic value of the focus group as an opportunity to provide a public relations channel for the recreation provider. Just by having focus groups, it is possible to increase awareness about the recreation opportunities in the community and publicize the survey, in turn increasing response rates to the final mail questionnaire. The outreach benefit obtained from focus group meetings needs to considered carefully when designing the focus group meetings. People who have an opportunity to attend the focus group meetings feel included in the data-collection process and could become strong supporters of a recreation agency. That support is often communicated to a larger network of people who belong to the same cohorts from which a focus group attendee was selected. For example, if a neighborhood association representative is invited to the focus group meeting, it is quite likely that the entire neighborhood would feel acknowledged by the recreation agency. The fact that focus groups are considered to be important outreach activities also becomes a problem for the agency. It is important for the organizer of the focus group meetings to recognize that the meetings could be considered to be very important by members of the community, and those who are not invited could feel slighted by the oversight. It is thus extremely important to carefully think about the different groups that could be potentially invited to meetings and ensure that all the eligible groups are included.

There are usually three different kinds of groups that can be used. First, there are gatekeeper/stakeholder groups made up of the staff and board members of the recreation agencies that were being studied. These people are usually easy to identify because they compose the core members of the recreation service in a community. These are people who could have been elected into office as in the case of the Parks Commissions and Parks Boards, and ensuring that the elected officials are in the meetings helps to garner the support of the people represented by the elected members. The members of these groups could also include special ad hoc committees that might have been appointed by the elected officials or local government administrators to oversee a special recreation-related project such as a comprehensive master plan. The ad hoc committees are often made up of people who have a special interest in local recreation and need to be included in meetings since these stakeholder groups often have the most amount of interest in the citizen data. The groups made up of the staff and board members provide useful information about the activities offered by the agency, and provide useful organizational and institutional information concerning the ways in which the recreation providers reach out to the community.

A second category of groups includes the special interest groups that represent particular recreation interests in the community. These groups can provide in-depth discussions about specific needs of the community in terms of specialized recreation and leisure opportunities. Members of these groups are often visible in public meetings lobbying for their specific agendas. It is important to include members of such groups in the focus group meetings because it offers an opportunity for the groups to share their specific needs in a systematic manner during the focus group meeting. It is also important to make sure representatives from all the possible special interest groups are included in the meetings to avoid any accusations of "bias," where a group might have felt ignored and thus becomes antagonistic toward the recreation provider.

Finally, there are randomly selected members of the community who could represent issues that might have not been addressed by the special groups. These members of the focus group meetings could provide information that is relatively unclouded by institutional or special interest concerns.

The method of recruiting the groups is largely decided by the nature of the groups. For the staff and board members, there are no separate recruitment efforts needed, because all staff and board members are usually invited to attend the group meetings. In some cases, I have worked with agencies where the total number of staff members was less than ten people, and I encourage that all staff members attend meetings to get the greatest amount of input in the process of designing a questionnaire. Sometimes it is also possible to create heterogeneous groups where both the elected members and the staff members are included in the same meeting. The special interest groups are sent letters of invitation to attend focus groups, and the general public can be informed about the group meetings by press releases that invite the members to attend the meetings. As in most focus group administration, there is rarely any specific need or effort to select a true random sample that would be representative of the entire community. It is not necessary to draw generalizable conclusions about the entire community from the information collected in the focus group meetings. Thus, it is more important to collect information from the people who can represent many different groups as opposed to collecting information from a random sample selected from the population.

The focus group meetings should be kept informal, and the role of the moderator is simply to facilitate the discussion. Usually only one moderator should direct the group discussion, but when the groups become larger than four to six people, a second moderator might be needed to assist in a useful discussion. The moderator has several tasks to accomplish within a period of about seventy-five minutes, which is the recommended length of the focus group meeting.

An important task of the moderator is to create an outline of issues to be discussed in the meetings. The issues can include general attitudes toward the recreation provider, assessment of specific current activities provided by the recreation provider, discussion of future needs for recreation activities, ways of financing such activities, and a closing discussion of any issues that the members of the group would want to address. These different issues are usually organized in the form of a set of broad and open-ended questions that the moderator can ask of the group. The questions need not be designed as a questionnaire, but are primarily a guideline for the key talking points. This document is often called the focus group protocol and should be prepared by the moderator prior to the meeting. It is an especially important document for those who are new at the job of moderating groups, because the protocol helps to keep the meeting on task and focused on the important issues.

Meetings can sometimes devolve into a session where the participants voice their special interests and present their grievances about the recreation agency. A skilled moderator helps to steer the discussion away from such issues and guides discussion back to the more important purpose of eliciting issues that can eventually translate to questions on the final questionnaire.

It should be noted that the groups operate best when the moderator is unbiased and does not appear to have a personal agenda that supersedes the purpose of the meeting. The moderator must act as an impartial researcher whose charge is to gather the information and process it into questionnaire items. Any indications of bias would quickly make participants wary of what they say in the meeting. Consequently, it is usually not a good idea to have senior leaders of the recreation agencies moderate the meetings. People such as directors and superintendents automatically are viewed as biased, rendering the group meeting ineffective. The moderator must also possess sufficient group communication skills to facilitate the meeting without taking on the role of a group leader. In fact, the moderator is not the leader of the group, but merely a person who ensures that the group operates in an efficient way. Yet, leisure research has shown that at least one of the moderators needs to have a clear grasp of the substantive issues of recreation to lead the discussion along useful channels focused on recreation issues and keep it from digressing too far from the subject. Researchers have pointed out that higher involvement of the moderator with the topic of discussion ensures that a desired set of topics are covered.

The success of the focus group administration in the area of leisure needs assessments also depends on the people who actually attend the meetings. There has to be ample interest in the community to provide input toward the needs assessments. Since the group recruitment is conducted on a purely voluntary basis with no incentive or coercion, the success of the groups depends directly on the level of interest and awareness in the communities. The recreation agency needs to spend sufficient time developing a comprehensive list of the potential participants and then starting with ample time to contact the participants and gain their cooperation. Typically only about half the number of people who are invited will actually attend the meeting. It is therefore important to start with a sufficiently large pool of people to get the appropriate number of people in the focus group meetings. There are numerous factors that can have impact the level of attendance. Weather and location of the meetings are two major items that contribute to attendance. People are much less willing to brave inclement weather to come to a meeting that requires them to volunteer their time. Similarly, people are less willing to travel long distances to attend a meeting. For example, when moderating focus group meetings in large and dispersed communities as in the case of a county-level recreation provider, it is recommended that the focus group meetings are conducted in places that are easy for the participants to attend, with the moderator travelling to the various locations to facilitate the meetings.

It is important to note that the process of conducting the focus group must result in some tangible outcomes. The most important outcome is the development of the questionnaire that includes items that were obtained from successfully completed meetings. The data from the questionnaire eventually becomes the reliable and statistical information that can allow a recreation agency to make general decisions. However, it is also important to note that the focus group meetings produce a good amount of in-depth information that can be used to gain an understanding of the specific needs of the groups represented by the participants. This information must be retained for many different purposes. First, this information becomes the record of the discussion that leads to the questionnaire. Future researchers find the record of the focus group discussions extremely important in understanding why a questionnaire might have included specific questionnaire items. The detailed record is also important in a second way, because that information could include input from groups that might not always show up for public meetings or at other opportunities for providing input. The fact that participants are carefully identified and invited offers a greater degree of diversity of opinions in the focus group meetings as opposed to public meetings, which are often attended by the people who have the most complaints.

It is important to point out the difference between public meetings and focus group meetings. Public meetings, the centerpiece for planning consultants, are often performance activities offering very little research value. The public meeting offers the perception of "collecting data" but is usually not much more than a theatrical device to offer the community a chance to feel involved. None of the rigor of focus group administration is available in the public meeting. As such, it is really important that recreation professionals do not accept the planner's public meeting as a substitute for the focus group meeting. In the end, if the recreation agency is interested in obtaining useful data, then public meetings should actually be avoided until reliable data can be shared with the public in a meeting so that members of the public can use that reliable statistical data to make informed choices, which is the backbone of an effective democratic system.

The next chapter describes the ways in which the focus group information becomes critical in the process of designing the questionnaire.

5

Asking Questions

The focus group meetings help to collect the basic information required to design an effective questionnaire for collecting citizen input. This process is followed by the step of designing the questionnaire (see Appendix A). It should also be noted that collecting citizen input is an interrelated activity, where every step is connected with the other and impacts the next step. The focus group meetings should be considered to be the first step in the process of asking questions.

There are three primary factors that play a role in the design of the questionnaire: (a) the kind of data-collection method that would be used, (b) the different kinds of questions that would be asked, and (c) the precise wording of the questions. The data-collection method usually has a significant impact on the way the questionnaire is designed, and it is important to address that briefly before examining the process of designing the questionnaire.

The methods of data collection can be divided into two broad categories. The first method involves the use of an intermediary who poses specific questions to the respondent and then records the answers. This method uses interviewers who must be trained in how to conduct interviews. Most often, interviews are conducted face to face or by telephone. Respondents do not usually get to see the questioner in these situations, and they only hear a question and possible responses to the question in the case of closed-end questions, and their responses are recorded either by hand by the interviewer or by a computer.[1]

The second form of data collection method involves the self-response system, in which the respondent receives the questionnaire and then responds to it by circling numbers, checking boxes, or writing out long answers to specific questions. The primary method used for this form of data collection has been the mail delivery system, where the respondent receives a questionnaire by mail and then has to fill it out and return it to a central address. The mail data-collection method has been supplemented by the use of the Internet as the way of sending and receiving electronic questionnaires. These methods of data collection depend to a large degree on the cooperation of the respondent and his or her willingness to complete the questionnaire in a timely fashion.

The significance of these two data-collection methods lies in the fact that they require two different kinds of questionnaire formatting. In the case of the interviewer questionnaire, the format is most suitable for the interviewer to read from, with the necessary indications for skipping from one question to another or maintaining a question flow that is appropriate for the specific respondent. In the case of the self-response questionnaire, much greater attention needs to be paid to the way in which the questions are laid out on paper and the specific directions given to the respondent to be able to answer the questions easily and without too much confusion. In the case of needs assessments and attitude and opinion surveys related to leisure, the primary method of data collection is indeed the self-response method. Consequently, we will focus here on the way the questionnaire needs to be laid out for that specific method.

Once the issue of method of data collection has been resolved, it is then necessary to decide upon the broad areas that need to be covered in the questionnaire so that all the goals of the survey are met. The specific questions emerge later in the process, but the broad goals are determined during the planning process. Following are the key areas that need to be covered in the attitude and opinion needs assessments:

Existing Level of Interest and Participation

This set of questions addresses the level of interest that the community members have in the existing facilities and activities of an agency. This requires an extensive examination of the various activities that are provided by the agency. These can either be organized in an alphabetical order or in some logical order such as "general activities," "fitness and exercise," "trips," etc., so that they seem logical to the respondent. These questions are designed to determine the current levels of interest and thus provide valuable baseline information to the planner.

Future Needs

A second set of questions should address the future needs and perceptions of the needs of the community. These could vary from need for future land acquisition to the desire for better maintenance of facilities. Here too, an extensive list has to be developed, and respondents can indicate their perceived level of need for each item in the list. Increasingly, there is a trend to also ask the community about how they would like to pay for the additions and renovations. This provides an element of realism to the questions, and the respondents need to think about the cost before they can produce a wish list.

Personal Opinions

There has been ample research on the ways in which personal opinion questions can be asked. It is now the convention to use specific opinion statements and then ask the respondent to indicate his or her level of agreement with the statements. The list of statements needs to be developed carefully and the wording of the statements must be clear and precise as will be discussed in the next section. The personal opinion section yields specific perception data that can then be correlated with other information collected in the survey.

Behavioral Information

These questions address how much time the community has available for leisure-related activities and when that time is available. Additionally, planners might be interested in finding out how often community members use any facility at all. This provides valuable usage databases on which it is possible to segregate the data into users and non-users. This section can include a question regarding the reasons for non-use of the agency's facilities and activities. These reasons often have to do with the lack of information about the agency. It is therefore a good idea to include in this section a question about the way(s) in which the community learns about the agency. Here too, a list can be developed and the community response obtained with respect to the various methods of information delivery. This is also the section where questions about competition can be included. This section thus provides a profile of the community and its leisure-related behavior.

Goals

There is an increasing interest in assessing the community's perceptions of the goals of a leisure-providing agency. With changes in society and popular culture, with emergent social concerns around youth violence, drug abuse, unsupervised children, endangerment of the environment, and a general decline in the quality of service in many industries, the public perception of the role and efficiency of leisure agencies is changing. Moreover, since needs assessments and attitude and opinion surveys are often parts of a large-scale planning process, it is useful to solicit the community's opinions about the long-term goals of an agency (see an example of a youth questionnaire in

Appendix B). A set of goal statements can be developed and provided to respondents for ranking.

Demographics

By convention, this is the last part of the questionnaire and includes questions about gender, age, and income. These three individual characteristics are essential to make planning decisions. Additionally, questions about marital status, income, and ethnicity can also be included. In most cases, it is advisable to use the categories used by the census so that comparisons can be made between the data collected in the attitude and opinion study and standard census data.[2] Additionally, this section can contain questions that seek information about the respondent's household in terms of number of adults in the household, number of children of various age groups, and length of residence in the community as well as location of residence in the community. This last piece of information can be collected with the use of a map where the respondent would indicate their location (see an example of a survey map in Appendix D). All of these pieces of information make up the valuable demographic data that is essential for the planning purposes.

Once these question categories have been formulated, it is time to construct the final questionnaire. This is the point where researchers have to decide on the specific kind of language that would be used in the questionnaire.

Questionnaire Wording and Formatting

An important decision needs to be made concerning the way questions are worded when choosing between open-ended question and closed-ended or multiple-choice questions. Open-ended questions ask the respondent a question that can be answered in several different ways. These are similar to "essay" questions in an examination, where no pre-defined answers are provided. Multiple-choice questions, on the other hand, provide a set of possible responses and the respondent can choose one (or more) of the possible responses. Since these questions provide an existing set of responses, the respondent is forced into one of the possible choices. Occasionally this "forced choice" is supplemented with the use of "other (specify)" questions, where the respondent need not choose from the existing response categories and can choose the option "other" and then specify the other choice. This strategy works well in questions about recreation activities, because some respondents might not find their activity of interest within the responses and can then write out their specific "other" activity interest.

In the case of the open-ended question, attention needs to be paid to the "openness" of the question and the multiple ways in which the question can be interpreted. Unless the respondents infer the same meaning from the questions, different respondents will have different kinds of answers. While variation is expected and natural in responses, this should depend on differences in attitude and behavior and not on the question wording or interpretation. The open-ended question also poses a significant coding problem, since the answers are diverse and no systematic method of attaching a numeric value to the responses can be developed prior to receiving responses. In most cases, the coding process involves elaborate coding schemes that attempt to find similarities between responses and then attach a numeric value to comparable responses. This is a cumbersome and time-consuming process and is often error prone and subject to the biases of the coders. Often this process results in unreliable coding, since multiple coders might have varying interpretations of the responses resulting in the need for tests of intercoder reliability, which, if low, can lead to the need for recoding.

The closed-ended question, on the other hand, does not pose such coding problems. They are often pre-coded with numbers, and these numbers often refer to specific and clear concepts resulting in little coding ambiguity. There are two broad kinds of closed-end questions that can be used in an attitude and interest survey. First, there are the questions that have their responses ordered in some fashion. These questions are particularly appropriate for the study of attitudes since they can capture a range of possible attitudes. These questions are often fashioned after the Likert scale, and are thus called Likert-type scales. These items often use a five- or a seven-point numbering system, where the lower numbers refer to the absence or negative presence of an attitudinal item while the higher numbers refer to the presence or positive attribute towards an attitudinal item. For instance, in a Likert-type five-point scale, the statement could refer to the safety in public facilities and the respondent could be asked to "strongly agree," "agree," be "unsure," "disagree," or "strongly disagree" with the concept expressed in the statement. Each of the five responses is given a numeric value, with "5" being attached to "strongly agree" and "1" being the value for "strongly disagree." Consequently, at the point of analysis, it becomes possible to compute a mean value for the scale and make some judgments about the aggregate feeling of the community; thus, a mean value of 4.5 would suggest that the respondents feel relatively safe in the facilities.

While these ordered questions could provide information about the extent of feelings and attitudes, there is often the need to elicit information about specific options that are available to the respondent. For instance, it is often necessary to look at the various ways in which information is disseminated by a recreation agency. In this case, one of the ways to find the information is to have the respondents check the options that are provided. Here the options do not fall on a continuum, and the average value would be meaningless since the numbers are merely labels. For instance, in asking about how the respondent gets information about an agency, the question could provide a set of options such as "newspaper," "quarterly brochure," or "flyers in schools," and these options could be numbered 1 to 3. However, a mean of 2.8 is irrelevant in this case, because the numbers do not measure the extent of any attitude but merely the presence or absence of an attribute. It should also become clear to the reader how this question lends itself to the use of the "other (specify)" option, as the researcher could easily have missed out on a possible source of information about the agency, and respondents can provide that information in the "other (specify)" line. Generally, the difference between open-ended and closed-ended questions are as follows:

Open-ended Questions

1. They elicit detailed information.
2. They empower the respondents offering them the opportunity to expand on their thoughts and responses.
3. They can probe deeper and are not restricted to specific options and responses categories.
4. They are very difficult to code.

Closed-ended Questions

1. They make coding easier since there are pre-determined response categories.
2. They appear less intrusive since the respondent does not have to divulge detailed information.
3. They are less empowering since the respondent does not get the opportunity to expand on specific issues.
4. They provide standardized and easily comparable results.
5. They can use standardized terms particularly in the response categories.
6. It is possible to ask a larger number of questions in the space restrictions of a questionnaire.
7. The responses of these questions are open to detailed statistical analysis.

Given these advantages and disadvantages of the two kinds of questions, it is common that most attitude and interest surveys use a combination of the open- and closed-ended questions, as they elicit different kinds of information. The closed-ended questions provide the information on issues that need to be coded and analyzed to test for statistical differences and correlation. Questions of internal, external, and construct validity can be tested with the closed-ended questions. On the other hand, the open-ended questions provide the opportunity to elicit detailed information from the respondent. Often the open-ended question could be as short and direct as "additional comments" that offer more detailed and specific questions that address specific needs, attitudes, interests, opinions, and behaviors of the respondents. However, once the combination has been determined, it is necessary to pay attention to the specific ways in which the questions can be worded and asked.

Factors to Consider in Questionnaire Design

The important issues are clarity, directness, parsimoniousness, and ease of interpretation. All the factors that make for effective communication are applicable in the case of the questionnaire. This is the primary form of contact between the respondent and the researcher/research team, and to gain the maximum benefit from this instrument, it has to appeal to the respondent and be easy for the respondent to understand and react to. In view of this, the following factors need to be considered when an instrument is being put together.

Will the Words Be Clearly Understood?

Often questionnaires use words that could be confusing, vague, unclear, and complicated. This can make it difficult to answer the question, as the respondent will not be able to interpret the question. In such case, a simpler word that is perhaps more conversational will make it more accessible to the respondent. The focus groups help in this respect because they often expose the exact terminology that is used in a specific community as well any specific linguistic patterns that the community has.

Are There Abbreviations Being Used in the Questions?

Sometimes questionnaire designers use unusual abbreviations and technical concepts that might be familiar to the agency staff but might be completely foreign to the community. For instance, a term such as "zero-depth pool" might mean a specific kind of a swimming pool to the agency planners, but when used in a question, the term should be clarified just as an abbreviation such as ADA (Americans with Disability Act) might be familiar in the trade, but might not be as clear to the community. In such cases, abbreviations should be explained (as demonstrated here) by providing the full form in parenthesis.

Do the Questions Seem Vague?

Sometimes the questionnaire designer is unclear about the specific issues he or she is interested in. There might be a general area of concern that planners decide to ask a question about. This often results in the production of a vague and ill-formed question that can mean multiple things to various respondents.

This is due to the fact that people interpret the same term in different ways depending on their personal experience. Most often, this vagueness is seen in the personal opinion questions where unclear statements are provided and the respondents would answer in different ways simply because they might interpret the terminology in different ways. An example of this can be found in questions about the perception of long-term goals of an agency. In this respect, a statement such as "the agency should be involved with social issues" is an example of an unclear statement, because the concept of "social issues" could vary widely between respondents. On the other hand, a set of examples in parenthesis can help to focus the question further, thus providing uniformity to the interpretation.

Another way in which vagueness creeps into questionnaires is in the construction of the response categories. In the closed-ended questions, the strength of the questions lies in how well defined the response categories are. Thus, it could be difficult to distinguish between terms such as "rarely," "occasionally," and "regularly," just as it is difficult to define these terms with respect to the use of recreation facilities. A more precise and better way to seek the frequency of attendance is to say, "about once a month," "about two or three times a month," "about once a week," and so on, thus focusing and narrowing the categories.

Does the Question Have Built-in Bias?

When agency staff conducts internally produced assessments, they have certain expectations and personal opinions about the issues they would like to find out about. This often leads to biased questions. These questions are worded in such a way that the respondent is forced to answer them in a manner that might not accurately reflect his or her feelings about the issues but they would respond in a way that might be "conventional." Similarly, biased questions lead the respondent to say what "the researcher wants to hear," thus making the responses not the true reflections of feelings and attitudes. Bias can happen in many different ways. For instance, the question might be biased toward a particular behavior. For example, when asking about the usage of agency facilities, questions that ask, "Hundreds of people attended the pools this summer, how many times did you attend?" obviously put the respondent on guard and can easily lead to a convention-based answer rather than an honest one.

Bias can also result in using overly positive (or negative) terms and definitions to describe behavior. Saying "There have been many injuries due to rollerblading. Do you think we need a new rollerblading facility" is less accurate than simply stating, "There is a need for a new rollerblading facility," in which the negative comment about rollerblading is simply removed. In most cases, bias can be removed by a careful review of the questionnaire by an outside group. Often bias is nonexistent in questions produced by independent researchers who come in as consultants in a community because they have fewer pre-existing notions and expectations about the community. The best way to reduce bias is to rephrase questions to take away unnecessary terms that could lead the respondent to answer in a leading manner. This is primarily a semantics issue, and by remaining objective, many of the problems of questionnaire bias can be avoided.

Does the Question Seem Objectionable?

Sometimes questionnaires contain items that might be unpalatable to the respondent. Most often, this applies to personal questions of behavior and demographics. Unless the respondent is given enough rationale, he or she might refuse to answer questions regarding private belief, behavior, and allegiances. For example, asking questions about sexual behavior in a recreation needs assessment will probably not yield responses from the community. Most often, potentially objectionable questions can be made less so by providing the context of the survey. In a community recreation needs assessment, there is no relevance for questions about sexual behavior, but a questionnaire about HIV/AIDS and associated risks might include questions about sexuality that can yield truthful responses. Similarly, questions about personal background, such as race, income, and religion can become objectionable questions since respondents might feel that such questions probe too deeply. However, in recreation studies, these are often important questions, and the best way to address these questions is by providing categories that are not too precise. For instance, instead of asking a respondent to report his/her annual income, it is better to provide a set of categories such as, "less than 25K," "26K to 35K," and so on, asking the respondent to indicate which group he or she belongs in. Such strategies often help to make the questions appear less intrusive and objectionable.

Does the Question Ask about Two or More Issues?

This is perhaps the most common problem with novice questionnaire writers. Very frequently, question items ask about two different but related issues, leading to confusion on the part of the respondent and ultimately resulting in unreliable data. This happens most often in the personal opinion questions unless the writer is particularly careful about avoiding them. For instance, a questionnaire item such as, "I feel that the agency is staff is courteous and well informed about leisure activities," might seem legitimate, but the respondent would be faced with a dilemma because courteousness and being well informed are two different attributes, and it is possible that one can be courteous and uninformed or vice versa. In such cases, the response becomes ambiguous and unreliable because at the end of the study, the planner will not be able to distinguish between the two concepts, leading to incomplete planning information. The simplest way to correct such double-barreled questions is to split them up into multiple questions, each addressing the specific construct the agency is interested in.

Is Too Much Knowledge Assumed?

In many cases, researchers assume too much about respondents. These could be assumptions about their level of knowledge, their behavior, and their overall awareness of the issues that the researcher is interested in. This could be damaging, leading to either inappropriate answers or missing information. This often happens in the case of leisure questionnaires because the authors of the questions are leisure professionals who might know a lot about this specific field. However, one must be careful that such knowledge does not lead to assumptions about the respondents, since the questionnaire goes to members of the community at large and many of these members would not know of the specific activities or even the existence of the leisure providing agency. Indeed, it is not unusual for up to 75% of a community to never have attended any leisure and recreation activity or facility provided by an agency. In light of this, any assumptions about the community could be detrimental to the survey. In asking questions about behavior, it is often necessary to find out the level and extent of a behavior to assess the need for a particular facility. In such cases, it is imperative that appropriate time references are provided to the respondent so that they can assess the extent of a behavior within a period of time. Additionally, such time references also provide the researcher with a better tool for the planning activities since they can project on usage over specific periods of time. Consequently, asking a question such as, "How often do you use the swimming pool?" yields much less information than asking, "How often have you used the pool in the past twelve months?" One has to be careful, however, about how precise and broad the time reference is. It is better to keep the reference broad enough so that an accurate assessment can be made about the period. Consequently, it is better to ask about a month than a week, just as it is better to ask about one year instead of three years. Similarly, it is better to ask about the "past month/year" rather than a specific period of time such as "between May 1, 1992 and April 30, 1993." Such specific time references make it difficult for the respondent to recall the exact time period. If indeed such questions need to be asked, then some references need to be provided such as "the year the Olympics were held in Atlanta, how often did you play basketball in the neighborhood park?" Here the respondent can relate back to a special event and answer the questions in a more informed manner.

Can the Responses Be Compared with Standard Information?

Perhaps one of the most frustrating experiences in conducting leisure needs assessments is to collect large amounts of information but still have little indication of the validity of the information. While responses about recreation behavior and attitudes can be guessed or assumed ahead of the study, it is possible to compare the demographic information with experience, particularly the census. However, to be able to do so, the response categories need to match the categories of the standard database. For instance, if the response category for age in census is "between x and y years," then the needs assessment should also use the "x" and "y" limits so that the results are comparable. Consequently, it is imperative that the standard information be consulted before writing the questions and collecting the data.

Once these issues have been resolved, it is possible to move on to the final stage of the process of creating a questionnaire where it is formatted in a specific way that makes it easy for the respondent. It is important to note that the way the questionnaire looks has a lot to do with how readily the respondent will answer it and send it back. Consequently, attention needs to be paid to a variety of issues ranging from ordering of questions to the amount of blank spaces provided in the questionnaire. The following are some of the conventions that can be followed.

The Questions Need to Be Ordered in a Logical Fashion

The order in which questions are presented impacts on the response rate. It is advisable to place personal demographic questions at the end of the questionnaire. This makes the questionnaire appear less intrusive. It is always a good idea to begin needs assessment questionnaires with a set of questions about leisure behavior where the respondent can simply indicate his or her behavior with respect to leisure and needs for specific recreation and leisure activities and facilities. This is often followed by personal opinion questions, which are slightly more intrusive. Within the personal opinion questions, it is often a good idea to place "reverse" questions. Sometimes respondents fall into a trend of either agreeing with or disagreeing with similar questions. Thus, a bank of questions about the safety and security of parks could elicit similar responses. However, if within such a bank of questions there is a question that would reverse the trend of responses, then the respondent is forced to pay attention to the questions and not fall into a repetitive trap. For instance, placing the statements "I feel safe in the parks," and "There is a high level of threat to security in the parks" next to each other would force the respondent to pay attention to the questions rather than simply responding with agreement or disagreement as it is unlikely that a respondent would agree to both the statements. If they agree to the first, then they would probably disagree with the second statement and vice versa. Thus, the ordering of questions has a lot to do with the way the responses are elicited. The personal opinion section is followed by the more personal questions about leisure time availability, personal demographics, and household information. This has been the convention in most questionnaires and increasingly people expect this pattern, thus making the questionnaire appear less intimidating.

The Questionnaire Needs to Be of Reasonable Length

In most self-response mail surveys, a long questionnaire is undesirable. Usually any questionnaire that is longer than eight to ten pages (8.5 inches by 11 inches page) long could find its way in the trash can. Long questionnaires are more demanding on the respondent's time and are consequently avoided. It is also possible to think of the questionnaire in terms of the time it takes a typical person to fill it out. Anything that takes more than 20 minutes is undesirable in the case of community needs assessments. Attention needs to be paid to keep the questions of reasonable length that does not become too demanding on the respondent.

The Questionnaire Should Be Easily Readable

Very often, in an effort to pack in a large number of questionnaire items within a reasonable number of pages, researchers are tempted to use minute print faces and clutter the questionnaire with too much printed information. This becomes a burden on the respondent since the questionnaire simply appears unappealing and confusing. It is thus a good idea to allow enough white space on the questionnaire with ample margins at the top, bottom, and sides and enough space between question items so that the material is easily readable. Sometimes techniques such as the alternative shading of lines are used to distinguish between question items. Efforts need to be made to make the instrument attractive to the respondent.

This is also connected with the issue of the cover letter. In most cases, mail surveys such as the community needs assessments are delivered by mail and are accompanied by a cover letter. This is the first piece of communication that the respondent encounters, and attention needs to be paid to this document so that it is appealing and a persuasive argument is made to convince the respondent to answer the questions. Additionally, the cover letter should stress the issues of confidentiality and anonymity when they apply. The cover letter should be signed by a recognizable public official and should be placed on an official letterhead to legitimize the survey to the respondent (see an example of a questionnaire cover letter in Appendix C).

All of these efforts provide the crossover between the questionnaire elements and the factors that are critical to the data-collection process. As indicated earlier, in most cases, the method of data collection used in the community surveys is indeed mail. The alternatives available to the agency are data collection by telephone interviews or by face-to-face interviews. Each of these methods has its strengths and weaknesses, but generally the mail data-collection system provides a cost-effective way of collecting information from the community.

Notes

[1] There is an increasing use of computers in these kinds of data-collection methods. Most professional survey organizations now maintain some form of Computer Assisted Telephone Interview (CATI) system, where the interviewers simply punch in the answers, thus producing a data set as the study progresses. In the case of face-to-face situations, interviewers are equipped with portable computers and they can use a Computer Assisted Personal Interview (CAPI) system.

[2] This is an important issue and is often missed by the planner. For instance, if the question of age is being asked and the age breakdown in the questionnaire is 17-21, 22-26, etc., they do not match the standard census categories making comparison impossible at a later time. It is much better to use the census categories when devising the questionnaire. This same principle applies to questions of ethnicity as well.

6

Collecting Data

Constructing the questionnaire is the principal initial phase of any needs assessment or program evaluation phase. The quality of the data is primarily dependent on the way in which the data collection is accomplished. In general, there are four primary modes of data collection. It is possible to collect the data using a face-to-face format, a telephone interview format, a mail data collection system or data collection using an electronic format, as in the case of the Internet. This chapter will explore the way in which each process is carried out and the benefits and drawbacks of each process. It is, however, important to note that there are situations when the methods can be combined to achieve the best results. One of the most important factors in achieving the best results deals with the notion of response rate. Unless the response rate is high, the data might not be of great value. Consequently, it is useful to consider this issue before looking at the various kinds of data collection and the details associated with each.

Response Rate

The key aspect of the data-collection process is ensuring a system that will yield the largest response rate. In explaining the idea, I use the example of mail data collection, because that is the most common method of collecting data used in leisure and recreation research. However, all the concepts associated with the mail process are applicable to the other forms of data collection. In all cases, a simple definition of response rate is as follows:

RR = (total completed questionnaires)/(eligible sample)

When multiplied by 100, it can be expressed as a percentage. The numerator is total number of completed questionnaires. Certain criteria need to be set to determine when a questionnaire is considered complete. First, a questionnaire can be considered complete if a certain portion of the questionnaire has been completed. This method is insensitive to which particular portions have been completed and focuses only on the fact that an agreed portion of questions were answered. A second approach uses a set of key questions strategically chosen within the questionnaire as the criteria for determining the completeness of the questionnaire. If all of the key questions were answered, the questionnaire would be considered complete. This is a far more stringent method for determining completeness and should be used whenever the research goals need specific questions answered. The researcher can also consider using a combination of these two approaches.

The denominator in the above formula refers to the total number of eligible members in the sample. Eligibility is a key criterion that needs to be well defined. Often eligibility depends on demographic attributes. If the population is defined by a particular age category, then only those members who are in that age category are considered eligible. Similarly, if only the people in a particular neighborhood are the definition of the population, then anyone outside of the neighborhood is ineligible. Usually, the sampling process attempts to eliminate any ineligible members by targeted sampling with respect to location, age, and other possible eligibility criteria. However, even in the most carefully selected sample, there could be some cases that are ineligible and they need to be removed at the time of computing the RR. For instance, in the case of a mail study, some of the envelopes mailed out could be returned by the postal system as undeliverable. Those should be considered ineligible. The following example will illustrate the way in which RR can be computed:

Total sample selected	**1,000**
Total returned by post office as undeliverable	**12**
Total considered outside of the geography by zip code	**350**
Total completed and geographically eligible	**475**
Total eligible (1,000-[12+350])	**638**
RR (475/638)	**74.45%**

It is important to note that simply dividing the total completed interviews (475) by the total sample (1,000) would yield a lower RR (47.5%), which would be an incorrect representation of the response rate. A low response rate indicates that a portion of the people who received the questionnaire did not fill it out and return it to the surveyor. This could mean that the non-responding members of the sample represent a section of population with common characteristics. However, on the other hand, if a large number of the non-respondents are ineligible, (i.e., not members of the population being studied), then their non-response is no cause for anxiety. As in the above example, out of the 525 members of the sample who did not respond, 350 were not even a part of the eligible population, consequently their lack of response is of little importance to the validity of the study.

Perhaps the biggest challenge to the agency/researcher conducting the mail survey is obtaining a "high" response rate. Just as the sample size is a nebulous number and is dependent on several competing factors (e.g., cost, allowable error etc.), the appropriate response rate is also dependent on many considerations.

Although the notion of the response rate is extremely important to the study, very few leisure and recreation surveys report their response rates. These numbers are often not clearly stated in reporting the results of a survey. However, a low response rate has two primary consequences that are specific in the case of leisure and recreation surveys and needs assessments. On one hand, low response rates introduce non-response error that is extremely difficult to compute or estimate. The computation and the correction of non-response error requires the imputation of the missing responses and making estimates based on the existing responses. This is an inaccurate process and can not really be applied in the case of missing responses. Consequently, a low response rate leaves the researcher guessing about the people who did not respond. In some cases, it is possible to argue that if the respondents are similar in demographics to the overall composition of the community then there is little fear that missing responses are significantly different. While that may be true, it is still an assumption at best, and the reasons for the non-response remain a mystery.

That is also the second consequence of a low response rate. Since the reasons for the low response remain unclear, it poses an image problem for the leisure organization. It can be argued that the very fact that there is a low response rate could be connected with the appraisal of the provider. For instance, in one needs assessment at a medium-sized midwestern city with an active recreation department, the first mailing yielded a response rate of 10%. Since such a low response rate was unacceptable, a second mailing was commissioned. However, it was interesting to note that one of the problems associated with the department was the lack of visibility. Although the department made significant contributions toward the enrichment of the leisure experience and opportunities, it failed to advertise these efforts well, which likely resulted in many residents not even understanding where the mailing originated and discarding it. Such low response rates also pose a political challenge for a tax-supported body such as a recreation department. In the end, the department is responsible to the people of the community, and their constituency can easily raise the questions of validity and reliability associated with such low response rates. When thousands of dollars of public money are spent in doing these surveys, an inadequate response rate can raise some very troubling and legitimate questions about the process. Thankfully, low response rates are not necessarily common, and usually response rates obtained in the mail data-collection process associated with the leisure and recreation studies can be as high as 25%.

One of the most important considerations that survey researchers have is finding strategies that would boost the response rate. Ongoing research suggests that there are some strategies that can be used to boost response rates. In general, these strategies include repetition of data-collection efforts and the offering of incentives to the respondents. The ways in which these two strategies are applied vary with the different modes of data collection and are discussed later. However, suffice to say that by attempting to reach people in a repetitive fashion can encourage respondents to eventually answer the questions. Similarly, by offering the respondent a reasonable incentive it might be possible to gain their cooperation in answering questions.

The different methods of data collection can be categorized by considering the (1) the communication technology of data collection, and (2) the communication strategy applied to data collection. The first criterion deals with the technology that is used to reach the respondent. Currently there are four primary technologies that are commonly used—face-to-face meetings, printed questionnaires sent by mail, questionnaires delivered electronically over the Internet, and the telephone. On the other axis, data collection can be divided by the communication strategies—self-response or interviews. Needless to say, some of the technologies are more conducive to self-response while others can only be done in the interview mode. Thus, any discussion of data collection needs to consider both these axes of differentiation.

Self-Response Versus Interviews

In the case of telephone and face-to-face method of data collection, there usually is the intervention of an interviewer in the data-collection process. The respondents do not have to read or see the questionnaire, but the questions are read to them, and they answer by selecting categories offered by the interviewer. The respondent has fewer burdens on him or her because the respondent does not have to pay too much attention to the way in questions are arranged and printed. Issues of readability disappears in this case, since someone else is reading the questions aloud for the respondent. This makes the interview process more amenable to conditions where the respondent could potentially have problems with literacy. There is thus a set of advantages to the interview process, and some conditions demand the use of the interview process.

Perhaps the biggest downside of the interview process is introduced by the interviewer. Unless the interviewers are good (there are hardly any studies with a single interviewer!) the data is unreliable. The two primary reasons for this unreliability arise from the fact that the introduction of the interviewers brings in a set of "human" variables that is nonexistent in the self-response process. First, there needs to be extensive training so that interviewers are sensitive to the way in which questions should be articulated so that all interviewers are asking the same question. Further, in the case of complex responses, the interviewers need to be trained to record the correct response. An example might be needed to clarify the issue. Say, for instance, there is a question that asks about the reasons why the respondent might not be a regular attendee of the recreation department's activities. Among the various pre-coded forced choices to the question are two responses: "The facilities are not safe" and "Getting to the facilities is difficult." Now consider a respondent who says "It is so unsafe, I can never get there." How should this response be recorded? In most cases, a probing question ought to be asked to see if the "it" refers to the facilities or the buses one uses to reach the facilities. If the latter is the case, it is of little relevance to the specific recreation survey, and the primary reason for non-attendance would be "Getting to the facilities in difficult." If the "it" refers to the facilities as well, then perhaps both the responses are legitimate (and it should be recorded as such, since these questions are often designed to accept multiple responses). However, with multiple interviewers, there needs to be some degree of "agreement" or "reliability" that the various interviewers would indeed interpret the responses in a similar manner.

A second issue connected with interviews is the fact that interviewers are often tempted to "interpret" a question for the respondent. While probing for clarification is a legitimate task of the interviewer, interpreting questions or response categories (unless they are well defined and standardized) leads to contamination of the data. For instance, a common question category is the level of interest in various activities provided by a recreation department. The possible response categories could be based on a five-point scale ranging from "Lots of Interest" to "No Interest." If a respondent were to say, "Oh, I go there once a month—would that be low interest?" the interviewer should not be answering the question but probing the respondent to clarify the response and put it in one of the five categories. This is important because different interviewers could answer the question raised by the respondent in different ways and thus yield different results. Some of these problems can be identified by observing the interview process, and later by computing inter-coder reliability to see the degree of agreement between the interviewers. Many of these problems disappear in the self-response questionnaire as in the case of a mail survey.

In the self-response questionnaire, the respondent is the one who would read and answer the questions. This requires specific literacy needs and makes it a burden on the questionnaire designer that the survey be well formatted so that the respondent feels the desire to answer the questions. This process also puts a burden on the respondent, because he or she will have to take the extra effort to take the questionnaire to the mailbox and arrange for its return. Although there are strategies to facilitate the process, it is still something the respondent has to do. On the other hand, there is little room for error in this process, because the respondent has the questions and categories laid out in clear terms. As long as the questions are readable at the level of the intended respondent, it has to be assumed that the respondent is truthful about the answers and was able to interpret the questions in a standardized manner.

However, these two remain the primary modes of data collection and there are several different questions that need to be asked when deciding on the mode of data collection. These include the following:

- Is the particular kind of research—its goals, population, and questions—suitable for a particular mode of data collection?
- Are there enough resources available to use the selected process?
- Is there enough time to complete the selected process?

The discussion of each of the modes of data collection will be built around these concerns and then the procedure will be discussed in some detail.

Telephone Interviews

As indicated earlier, in situations where the respondent cannot be sent a self-response questionnaire, one could consider a phone survey. If the researcher is interested in asking sensitive questions about private matters then it is important to establish a sense of trust between the researcher and the subject. This can be done more readily by phone or face to face. For example, it is possible that by matching the interviewer with the respondent (e.g., male interviewer with male respondent) a high level of candor can be obtained that might lead to the option of asking questions that might not be possible to include in a mail questionnaire.

Phone data collection costs more per completed interview but can be finalized and implemented faster than mail data collection, but usually not as quickly as collecting data using the Internet. The higher cost is associated with the technology, the cost associated with paying interviewers, and the cost of supervising the interview process. As pointed out in the earlier section, the success of the interview lies in the way in which the interview was conducted. There are thus significant costs associated with these basic resources required to do phone data collection. Finally, in terms of expected response rate, phone data collection yields a greater response rate than the mail process and about the same response rate as in the case of the face-to-face interview.

Finally, there is a set of increasing concerns about the use of telephones for survey data collection. The concerns are both related to the interpersonal communication aspects of the phone data-collection process as well as the changes in the technology of telecommunication. At the interpersonal level, the American population, in general, is getting to be "over surveyed." With the increasing awareness about the need to conduct consumer surveys and market analysis, as well as the ease with which listed phone numbers can be obtained, more households are getting phone calls from people conducting surveys. This can lead to an increasing resistance to phone interviews. Almost to challenge this increasing tendency for phone solicitation, American households now have available a variety of technological gadgets to control the flow of phone calls. Survey researchers are increasingly frustrated by the high incidence of answering machines connected to phone lines. Often the answering machine can be used as a call-screening device, and phone interviewers might never have access to an adult in the household to conduct an interview. Other technological options such as caller identification also add to the potential respondent's ability to refuse to complete an interview. In addition, there are laws in the United States that allow an individual to request exception from phone interviews and solicitation (often called the Do Not Call List), which could make some phone data collection illegal. The resources required to do phone data collection are also influenced by the ease with which phone numbers can be obtained.

Who to Call

The obvious place to start is to use the local telephone book, which unfortunately presents many problems. First, they are often dated. Telephone books are published only once a year, but telephone numbers are issued, changed, or withdrawn across the entire year, so there is always a section of the population who would not be included in the listing. Consequently, these people have a zero probability of being included in the study. The second problem also deals with omission, but here the concern is with voluntary omissions, where members of the population request that their phone numbers not be listed in the phone book. While the first concern about the phone book being a dated list can be less problematic since it can be argued that there is no necessary pattern in the movement of people and the issuance of new phone numbers, the second concern over unlisted phone numbers is more alarming, because it can be argued that some specific categories of people are the ones who choose to have their numbers left out of the phone book. For instance, it is not unusual to find that single women living by themselves, doctors, lawyers, and other professionals choose to have their numbers left out of the phone book. Needless to say, the loss of these people from the study can have an effect on the validity of the community data. Additionally, this tendency has continued to grow, and in larger metropolitan areas, the unlisted rate can be as high as 35% to 40%, suggesting that such a large section of the population is being kept out of the data-collection process.

There can be a relationship between social and economic characteristics and telephone coverage. Particularly in larger cities, it is often the case that the issuance and withdrawal of telephone numbers is connected with the ability to afford a telephone connection. Consequently, when phone numbers are disconnected, it might be related to demographic issues that are of critical importance to the recreation provider.

Finally, phone books do not list mobile phone numbers, and as more people rely solely on mobile phones, the usefulness of the phone book is rapidly diminishing. Studies that rely on pre-existing lists of phone numbers simply cannot be trusted, and the data should be considered unreliable for all planning purposes.

In light of these issues, the only reliable data that is collected by phone should come from a system where the phone numbers are randomly generated. This is an expensive process that helps to reach a larger cross-section of people. The procedure rests on the assumption that phone numbers are issued in a sequential manner. For example, if there is a prefix (the first three digits of the seven-digit phone number) 123, then the phone company usually begins to issue phone numbers starting with 123-0000 and attempts to fill the 10,000 numbers before moving on to another prefix (it is, however, not true that the next prefix would necessarily be 124). However, there are often holes within this numbering scheme, with a set of numbers missing (e.g., it might be that 123-0002 and 123-0004 do not exist), but by and large, there is an attempt on the part of the phone company to fill the number in these banks of thousands. Given this fact, it is possible to identify the prefixes in a city and then randomly select a set of four numbers knowing that since the prefix exists, it is possible that there are phone numbers within that prefix. Therefore, if a city has five prefixes, and a sample of 1,000 is desired, it is possible to select 200 strings of four-digit random numbers and produce the sample of phone numbers. While in theory this is a sound process, in practice this could be a nightmare, because after the selection has been completed, the researcher could find that none of the numbers actually exist because by chance only non-existing numbers were selected. This would mean a return to the drawing board and re-selection of the phone numbers. This process is often called Random Digit Dialing (RDD). However, because of the problems associated with the pure four-digit RDD process, there have been modifications made to the selection process. The two-digit RDD is the most popular form of selection. In this case, the phone book is first used to select a string of phone numbers; this is followed by the randomization of the last two digits of the phone number, by replacing the last two digits with a two-digit string of random numbers. For instance, if the selected phone number is 123-4567, then the randomized number could be 123-4578 where the "67" has been replaced by "78." This process increases the probability of finding a working number at the randomized location since the number not only uses the prefix, but also uses the first two digits of an existing phone number, thus making it more likely that there could be another working number in that bank of numbers. In other words, if 123-4567 is a working number, then it is much more likely that 123-4578 will also be a working number than 123-

3489 would be. The two-digit RDD thus reduces the likelihood of reaching non-working numbers, and increases the possibility of reaching numbers that are not included in the phone book.

The biggest drawback with the RDD process is the fact that it leads to the dialing of non-working and non-residential numbers. In most surveys related to questions of leisure and recreation, the attempt is to reach households to gain an understanding of the attitudes and opinions concerning leisure. Consequently, reaching non-residential numbers is useless. However, the RDD process leads to the generation of non-residential numbers causing unproductive dialing. In most metropolitan RDD samples, it is likely that about 40% of the numbers selected in the RDD process will be non-working, and only about 60% of the working numbers will be residential. Therefore, if one were to select a sample of 1,000 phone numbers by a RDD process, it is possible that only about 360 of these numbers are actually working residential numbers. But these residential numbers include the numbers that were not listed in the phone book and the researcher and the agency is assured that a representation of the population will be obtained. This also suggests that careful attention need to be paid to the anticipated percentages of non-working and residential numbers in a community. Those communities have larger portions of population who are unlisted and larger proportions of businesses will have to start with larger sets of phone numbers. Additionally, it is important to remember that the sample has to be bolstered to account for unreachable phone numbers, computer numbers, facsimile numbers, and other such numbers where an interview cannot be attempted. The RDD thus requires a large number of dealings adding to the cost of the study.

There is one common alternative to the RDD process when designing a telephone data-collection process. The Mitofsky-Wakesberg process (developed by Mitofsky and Wakesberg) requires the maintenance of accurate and careful record of the outcome of dialing to eliminate banks of phone numbers that have a lower likelihood of producing residential phone numbers. For example, if it appears that a majority of numbers in the 123-45XX bank of numbers are business numbers, then it makes sense to stop calling numbers within the 123-45XX bank. This determination is done in a step-wise fashion and is a complicated process, and if it is done without enough care, it can easily be reduced to a poorly conducted straight two-digit RDD process. However, with the increasing use of phone surveys, the Wakesberg process has gained a lot of attention; unfortunately, most such processes are not conducted in the rigorous manner developed by Mitofsky and Waksberg, and that description is used loosely.

Once the sample has been selected and the phone numbers identified, it is possible to work out the details of the data-collection process.

Hiring and Training Interviewers

Given the fact that the success of the phone interview is directly dependent on the quality of the interviewer, it is imperative that an agency spends enough time to find professional interviewers. As a rule, it is better to avoid the use of the recreation and leisure department staff to conduct the interviews. Even if the questionnaire is written in an unbiased manner, those involved with the survey can inject biases into the data-collection process that could contaminate the data. For instance, if the parks supervisor is involved with the telephone interview process, the questions concerning the parks would have special significance to the person, and unforeseen (or planned) biases can be introduced that would make the data unreliable if the supervisor probes the respondent too much to obtain a favorable response. Consequently, it is critical that interviewers be hired from a pool of people trained to conduct phone interviews. With the increasing use of telephones for data collection, it is now possible to find, particularly in lager metropolitan areas, people who might have developed an impressive range of experiences in interviewing. However, in all cases, certain criteria need to be kept in mind when hiring interviewers. Agency administrators in charge of hiring interviewers should consider the following parameters:

- Ability to read the questions clearly and fluently. Particularly in cases where the interview might be conducted with special hearing difficulties (and in a community survey, it is likely that a proportion of the sample will be that way), or with people who might not follow the language well,
- A quality of voice that is distinct and well articulated, particularly when heard over the phone,
- A quality of voice that does not greatly interfere with other interviewers who could be working in close proximity in an interview center,
- Ability to "ad lib" and respond to questions posed by the respondent. Although there are specific scripts set up to respond to the standard questions, there might be occasions when the interviewer will have to respond to special questions raised by the respondent, and
- Ability to generate some degree of camaraderie with the respondent so that the respondent would be willing to stay on the phone and complete the interview.

When these conditions can be found in an interviewer, it is likely that the person will require less training and will be able to begin to conduct interviews smoothly from the beginning.

Some training, however, needs to be considered since the interviewer would be dealing with a specific topic area that he or she might not be familiar with. In such cases, it is important that the interviewer receive some orientation regarding the questions being asked and the general area of recreation and leisure and the terms associated with the industry. This is study-specific training, and with good interviewers, this should be ample preparation. It is, however, advisable that some form of training manuscript be developed that the interviewer can reference after the training is over and the fieldwork begins. Finally, a question-by-question (q-by-q) training of the interviewer is imperative so that the person is clear about the exact wording of each of the questions, the response categories, the logic of the organization, and the reason the particular question is being asked. Q-by-Q training should never be circumvented, and often the initial time investment helps to save a lot of time later in the process.

While the interviewers are being hired and trained, it is possible to develop some of the procedures and protocols that are to be followed when the telephone interview is being conducted.

Setting Up the Phone Call Protocol

In the case of leisure and recreation surveys, it is advisable that independent interviewers be hired to conduct the interview. However, unless the interviewers already belong to a telemarketing or similar organization, they will have to be provided a space from where the phone calls can be conducted. Additionally, it is better to hire one or more supervisors who would be responsible for overseeing the data-collection process.

Centralization is the key to the resolution of the space question. Interviewers should be provided a central place with multiple phone lines so that they can all be observed and supervised at the same time. While the centralization process can lead to some degree of interference between the interviewers, these issues should be addressed in the training and planning. It is not a good idea, for instance, to seat all the interviewers around a seminar table in conference room with multiple telephones. It is necessary to provide each person with a small desk and some degree of privacy, perhaps with portable dividers often used to create cubicles. This provides the privacy and allows the supervisor to ensure that the interviews are being conducted in the correct way. What should be avoided are arrangements where interviewers can conduct surveys from their home or even spread out across an agency office sitting in different rooms. Such separation and distance from the supervisor can lead to spuriously implemented interviews, as well as frustration on the part of the interviewer if he or she does not have easy access to a supervisor who can answer questions.

Once the placement problem has been resolved, it is necessary to decide on the time of the interviews. In most general population surveys, it is better to use the evening hours to conduct the survey. The daytime hours are often unproductive, because many households will have no one at home. However, some amount of daytime calls need to be conducted in the early part of an RDD survey to eliminate the working non-residential numbers from the sample pool. Consequently, it is important to schedule interviewers in such a way that the bulk of the phone calls can be conducted in the evening. Once the phone call has been made and someone answers the phone, it is then possible to decide whom to interview. In most cases, the "the most recent birthday" method is used, where the interviewer would ask the respondent to list the persons living in the household by their birthdays, and then the adult over eighteen with the most recent birthday is selected for the survey.

It is, however, important to recognize that reaching the household could be a long and laborious process. In many cases, the respondent will refuse to participate in the interview; in other cases, an answering or fax machine might be reached, and sometimes the call may simply result in a busy tone. Indeed, many possible dispositions can result from a call. In some cases, these are final dispositions, and the phone number can be dropped from the list. For instance, if on the first call attempt, a recording is reached saying that the number has been disconnected, then it is safe to drop it from the list without the need for a follow-up call. If, on the other hand, the first attempt results in a busy tone or a refusal, then provisions need to be made to call the number back. It is critical that some standardized criteria be set up about this call-back process. For instance, if there are no standards set up, and if one interviewer decides to call each number only once, and another tries the number until an interview is completed (albeit with an irate respondent), then there is an automatic bias introduced into the process. The first interviewer might have reached a cooperative member of the population who might have had some experience with the leisure and recreation department, while the other interviewer was able to obtain a much different representation of the community. To avoid such pitfalls, it is necessary to determine the number of call backs that would be attempted.

In most "quick and dirty" phone surveys, as shown on television following campaign speeches, State of the Union addresses and political debates, no callbacks are attempted. A number is tried once, and if no response is elicited, then it is not called back. This is not the process that is advisable in the case of more carefully conducted surveys, the results of which can have far-reaching planning and policy implications. On the other end, research organizations are involved in sensitive surveys about health, social behavior, and crime, where it is imperative that every member of the population has a fair chance of being reached. In such cases, it is not unusual to see up to ten callbacks to reach the respondent. Clearly, there is a significant difference between one and ten callbacks as far as the response rate is concerned. In the first case, the response rates are dismal (although the pollsters rarely report the response rate, but simply report the sampling error, which provides incomplete information) the latter produces response rates of up to 97% and 98%. Thus, the agency commissioning its own telephone survey of the community would need to decide on the number of callbacks. The common industry standard for local government agencies varies between three to five callbacks (or four to six attempts for each number). After the set number of callbacks, the telephone number would be given a final disposition and removed from the list.

As should be clear from this discussion, with a sample size of 1,000 and allowing for four callbacks, there is the need to keep good records of the ongoing disposition of each phone number. Often, the same interviewer would not necessarily recall the same phone number, so all interviewers would need to know the disposition of a number at the beginning of a new shift. If the disposition is such that the respondent has refused twice, the supervisor might need to assign the number to a more experienced interviewer in an attempt to convert a persistent refusal. On the other hand, there could be situations where the respondent has said that he or she should be called back at a particular time or could have actually set up an appointment. Such special requests from respondents should be honored. Consequently, it is necessary to keep good records of the call outcomes. The availability of Computer Assisted Telephone Interview (CATI) systems make it simpler to keep these records. These systems could vary from simple computer routines that allow the recording of the responses on a standard data base system to more complex, multisystem networked programs that allow for greater complexity. It is important for the agency to be aware of these systems, because these can often make the interview process more efficient and less error prone, because the interview and the data entry are happening simultaneously.

The other type of data collection that we will examine in depth is the most popular form of data-collection process used in leisure and recreation surveys, mail data collection.

Mail Data Collection

Compared to the telephone process, mail data collection is a self-response system where there is no interaction between the respondent and the agency. Indeed, the respondent receives the material in the mail and is expected to simply complete the questionnaire and send it back. Needless to say, this can be a tricky process, because the respondent might feel little incentive to participate in the process. Moreover, there are no "refusal converters" to cajole and charm reticent respondents. Consequently, obtaining a good response in a general population mail survey often requires the production of a well-formatted and attractive questionnaire that is easily read and is free of complications. In such cases, the respondent might pay more attention to the questionnaire and feel like responding to it rather than disposing of it.

The Initial Mailing

The way in which the mailing is conducted often helps to boost the response rate. Agencies should always consider doing a first-class personalized mailing where the name of the respondent appears in the address label. Too often, people in households receive direct mailings addressed to "resident," and such mailings automatically find their way to the wastepaper bin. A personalized mailing often has a greater probability of being attended to. The questionnaire itself needs to be simple and accessible as indicated in the previous section. Along with that, the cover letter needs to make a clear appeal to the respondent as to why it is important to complete the questionnaire and return it. The cover letter often plays a critical role in this process. If an agency that is highly visible in the community is attempting to gather information about community needs, then a cover letter signed by the agency director might be recognized and elicit a good response. On the other hand, in large metropolitan areas where the specific administrators are not household names, it might be better to have the cover letter signed by the city mayor. In that case, the respondent might feel a greater urge to return the questionnaire.

The return process should also be as simple and effortless as possible. This means that there should be a postage-paid, self-addressed return envelope that accompanies the survey. Often the questionnaire can be designed in such a way that the respondent merely completes the instrument, folds it, and puts it back in mail. The key is to make the entire process simple and easy without placing undue burden on the respondent and without creating any hurdles for the respondent (such as requiring the respondent to buy a stamp to send the questionnaire back). These procedures on the first mailing often help to get an initial crop of returns.

The mailing itself needs to be coordinated in a way that all the respondents receive the questionnaires at about the same time. If the mailing list consists of 8,000 or 10,000 addresses, this could be a formidable task, because it would involve the insertion of that many packets with the questionnaire and the return envelope, sealing the outgoing envelope (see example in Appendix E) and carrying them to the post office. These tasks can be contracted out at relatively low costs, and that is sometimes the best option for an agency. However, it is important to ensure that the mailings do happen in a short period of time so that there is no bias introduced due to people receiving the mailing at different times.

If the strategy is to use a single mailing of the questionnaire, then the data-collection process concludes here and the agency has to wait and see how many among the sample return the completed questionnaire. Depending on the quality of the questionnaire and the amount of interest about the issues in the community at large, the response rate on a first mailing could vary between 10% to 35%. If the response rate is over a quarter percent, it is possible to consider that to be adequate and continue with data analysis from that point. If the response rate is lower than 25%, it is necessary to consider other strategies to boost the response.

Follow-up

Typically, the single mailing can be followed by mailing a reminder postcard to the entire list (see example in Appendix F). This can be done within two weeks of mailing the original questionnaire. The postcard simply thanks recipients for completing the questionnaire, if they have done so, or reminds non-respondents to fill out the questionnaires and put them back in the mail. Usually this is enough incentive to get some non-respondents to cooperate. The postcard can then be followed in two weeks by a second postcard. Generally, reminders are useful in boosting the response rate.

Variations of this can be tried with an intermediary phone call to replace the postcard. There are two key considerations in using the phone reminder. First, this assumes that working phone numbers are available for all members of the sample. This will likely not be the case, since people are increasingly unlisting their phone numbers and phone numbers often tend to change before they are updated in the phone book. Additionally, it can be very tedious to collect phone numbers of thousands of sample members unless it can be found electronically and printed out in a usable format. The second concern with phone follow-ups is the extent of information that can be shared/obtained in a phone follow-up. It makes little sense to contact a potential respondent on the phone merely to remind him or her to send in a questionnaire that could easily have been misplaced. If it is possible to find a potential respondent, then it is far better to obtain a completed interview from the person answering the phone because he or she is part of the original sample. This suggests the phone follow-up could evolve into a phone interview. Consequently, the person making the reminder phone call needs to be cross-trained as a telephone interviewer so that reliable data can be collected from people who agree to participate in the phone interview. There are also tools available that make automated phone calls that either leave messages on answering systems or have a machine-generated voice reminding the person answering the phone to complete the questionnaire. These automated systems are marginally useful because most people do not like to receive them and they are more influenced by phone calls from a real human being.

These procedures help to boost the response rate so that any bias associated with non-response error can be minimized. However, other than these mailing procedures, another important way to increase response rates is to simply increase community awareness about the ongoing survey.

Promoting the Study

Community surveys are unlike surveys of special populations where the population might have some intrinsic interest in the issue being surveyed. For instance, data collection from professional groups such as doctors, lawyers, university professors, or leisure professionals are often less complicated because the groups might have some degree of interest in the subject of the survey and also often feel responsibility to respond to the questionnaires. Consequently, there is a lesser problem of low response rate. In the case of the general population, with a mail survey of recreation needs and opinions, there is no necessary or compelling reason why recipients of the survey would feel compelled to return the questionnaire. Consequently, generating some degree of "hype" in the community is a good way to produce the necessary interest. This can be done by placing newspaper stories about the survey, putting out press releases, inserting information about the survey in the general mailing of the agency brochure, and by stories in local and community radio and television stations. These methods produce a certain degree of awareness of the survey and of the agency so when questionnaires reach the community, people will pay greater attention to them.

The response rate is thus dependent on a variety of factors that are impacted by every stage of the survey. Incorrect definition of population and sloppy sampling could have an effect on the response rate because some people receiving the sample could simply be ineligible, and if that rate of ineligibility cannot be determined, then a lower response rate would be reported. The response rate is also dependent on the various factors of questionnaire wording and layout. All the factors discussed about appropriate questionnaire construction help to increase response rate. The focus group discussions should also be used to assist in increasing response rate by seeking the assistance of the focus group participants to talk to their communities and encourage their friends, neighbors, and groups members to respond to the questionnaire when they get it. Consequently, the response rate is not simply dependent on the number of mailings or the nature of the follow up; it is dependent on a network of factors that all build up to the final conduct of the survey.

Finally, the concern with the response rate is primarily due to the fact that it might be true that non-respondents are similar in some fashion and the lack of response from this possibly homogeneous group could lead to a high level of non-response error. To a certain degree, comparing the results from the respondents with standard census information can test this proposition. If the census reports that the percentage of African-Americans in a community is 15% and the needs assessment shows that only 5% of the respondents are African-American, there is certainly a problem of non-response error since the African-American section of the sample did not respond. In such cases, new mailings could be needed. This needs to be anticipated as early as possible, and special efforts need to be made where lower response rates can be expected.

Alternative Forms of Data Collection

While the telephone interview and the mail data collection represent the two primary forms of data collection employed in community-wide surveys for leisure and recreation needs and evaluation, there are other forms of data collection that can also be attempted. The most common of the alternative forms is face-to-face collection.

Face to Face (f to f)

In the f-to-f scenario, trained interviewers are sent to houses where they conduct interviews. In some cases, a procedure similar to CATI, called Computer Assisted Paper and Pencil Interviews (CAPI), is used by interviewers to directly record the responses onto a computer system to assist in the data-entry process. It is expected that interviewers will return to the households a predetermined number of times (much like the callbacks in the phone data collection) before considering a dwelling unit to have been finalized. Given the direct contact with households, f-to-f interviews often yield response rates that could be as high as 97% to 98%.

Several conditions make the expensive method of f-to-f data collection attractive. First, f-to-f data collection becomes the most effective form when data collection has to be conducted from a cluster of people. If it is known that a section of the population is concentrated in a particular geographic location, then it makes sense to send f-to-f interviewers to such locations and collect data in the locations.

Since f-to-f data collection requires an interviewer, it offers a second benefit that needs to be noted: It is possible to match the interviewer's characteristics with those from whom data is being collected. For example, most American cities have neighborhoods that have higher concentrations of minority populations. These are the segments of the population who might not have permanent addresses or a phone numbers and very often, these are the people who are unable to voice their opinions through the more formal channels of telephone and mail data collection. In these situations, face-to-face data collection is perhaps the only effective data-collection procedure to use.

A third situation where f-to-f data collection is the best procedure is when data collection needs to be supplemented by other collections such as physical samples or the collection of opinions and attitudes needs to be corroborated with descriptions of the household that can only be obtained by observation. This is the reason why many medical surveys are conducted f-to-f, since the opinion data often needs to be supplemented by the collection of physical evidence such as blood or other bodily fluids. There have been surveys where the interviewer was accompanied by a trained phlebotomist who followed up the interview with the collection of a blood sample. This might not arise too often in the case of leisure and recreation surveys, but it is an example of special conditions when the f-to-f method seems most appropriate.

The primary disadvantage with the f-to-f method is cost. Given the fact that interviewers have to travel to the locations and often go back a number of times, the f-to-f method is an expensive data-collection process. It also takes longer because there is more work involved including the time it takes to get to a location. These two factors need to be kept in sight when thinking of the f-to-f process.

Electronic Data Collection

The popularity of the Internet has had a significant impact on data-collection strategies used by many organizations. Parks and recreation agencies have rapidly adopted digital tools for collecting citizen data. There are two primary modes by which this is done. On one hand, it is possible to use the World Wide Web (Web) to create questionnaires that can be made available to respondents so that the respondent has to visit a website to answer questions. In this case, the respondent must be willing to voluntarily visit a website where the individual can complete the questionnaire. The other method involves sending a digital questionnaire to the respondent who simply has to respond to the questions sent to the person by electronic mail. The respondent does not have to make any special effort to answer the questions since the instrument is sent to the person.

In either case, there are some important things to consider about the process of collecting data using an electronic or digital questionnaire. In order to achieve these benefits, it is important to follow a set of steps to attain the best result. As in the case of other data-collection methods, significant effort needs to be put in the development of the questionnaire. Just because the questionnaire is being administered on the Web does not imply that the development of the questions would be any simpler. It is, however, possible to customize the questionnaire much more easily with the Web-based data-collection process because it is simple to create multiple versions of the same questionnaire with minor differences between the versions. Thus it might be possible to develop five different questionnaires, each customized to specific facility or category of programs.

Next there must be care taken in programming the questionnaire for digital distribution. While a questionnaire may look fine on paper, when transferred to the Web it is necessary to ensure that it looks good on the computer screen. The questionnaire also needs to be user friendly and easy to navigate on a variety of different Web browsers. There thus needs to be significant testing of the Web questionnaire before it is ready for data collection. The programming process is not a simple one, and dedicated personnel are needed who are able to create an attractive questionnaire that will yield a high response rate.

The actual contact with the population that would be completing the questionnaire has to be planned carefully. This is especially true for data collection on the Web, where the respondent must voluntarily visit a website to complete the questionnaire. Typically there are two ways in which respondents could be invited. The first way is to invite people to visit the website where the questionnaire is located and complete the survey. This requires the availability of some contact information, preferably e-mail addresses, of the people to whom an invitation can be sent (see an example of a reminder e-mail in Appendix H). Alternatively, it is possible to mail a letter or postcard asking people to visit the website to complete the questionnaire. If, however, no contact information is available, then the second possible method involves widely advertising the location of the questionnaire through traditional means of marketing. Information about the location of the Web site can be included in the printed and broadcast media where the potential respondent could get the information about the online questionnaire at offline sites. This makes the questionnaire available to a wide group of respondents, and thus it is possible to collect broad-based data. Depending on the purpose of the study, it is certainly possible to mix these strategies to attain the highest reach. Also, facilities such as public computer terminals and computer kiosks located in recreation centers and libraries could be used by respondents to complete the web-based survey.

There is little doubt that this mode of data collection will become the wave of the future. There are, however, some significant limitations to this method based on the availability of contact information of a population and the level of access that the population might have to the tools required to complete the questionnaire. If the goal is to do a general population study, it could be very difficult to gather reliable contact information in the form of e-mail addresses that can be used as the starting point for creating a true random sample (see chapter 7). When such information is unavailable and the data-collection Web site is made open to the public at large then it is possible that the quality of the data is not generalizable because it is impossible to be sure that the data has not somehow been biased. There will always be an element of bias in Web-based data collection. Sometimes this bias is not considered a problem as in the case of customer satisfaction studies. In such studies, the goal is to collect information from a special group of people who are in a particularly unique position to comment on a recreation program or facility. If e-mail addresses of users are available, then it is relatively simple to conduct a Web-based data-collection process with such special groups.

Once it is clearly understood that digital data collection has its specific limitations, and if the method is used appropriately, then it does provide a set of unique opportunities and benefits. As indicated earlier, several different questionnaires can be fielded at the same time because there are few limitations on size of the questionnaire and the amount of data being collected. Generally, it is relatively inexpensive to do digital data collection because the costs related to placing the questionnaire on the Web and data collection and data entry are far lower than other modes of data collection because there is no copying, mailing, or data coding and entry involved. In a sense, the respondent does the data entry by simply completing the questionnaire. It is also possible to do rapid data collection using the digital method. Once the questionnaire is made available on the Internet, people can begin to respond immediately. Furthermore, there is no delay in data analysis as Web-based surveys can be used to gain immediate feedback because there is no data entry time required. Because the questionnaire only has a digital presence, it can also be modified as needed. Unlike mail and telephone questionnaires, which are far more difficult to change once they have been mailed or programmed into computer-aided telephone interviewing tools, the Web-based questionnaire (example in Appendix G) offers much more flexibility, particularly when data is being collected over a length of time. The lack of data entry delay and the availability of integrated analysis tool make the data available as soon as a person completes the questionnaire.

There are many benefits to each form of data collection just as each method has associated burdens and problems. It is thus useful to consider the ways in which different methods can be correctly combined with each other to achieve the highest data quality.

Combining Methods

A key issue to keep in mind is that these different methods are not necessarily watertight. In other words, a well-designed survey could use multiple methods to get the best representation and response rate without unduly increasing costs. A combined method could begin with a mailing of questionnaires with the option of an electronic response to an Internet address. After about two weeks, the non-responders (both mail and electronic mail) could be reached by a follow-up phone call and an interview conducted with the ones who can be reached by phone. This process would also yield a list where the respondent could not be reached by phone, but the post office did not return the envelope as undeliverable suggesting that it is a deliverable address without a phone. All or some of such members of the sample can then be reached for a f-to-f interview. This procedure would ensure wide coverage, and with appropriate numbers of callbacks and returns to the households, a good response rate could be achieved as well.

Needless to say, this would be an expensive procedure as well, and very often the entire data-collection process ends up being a compromise between response rate and cost. While a concerted approach such as the above could yield a high response rate, agencies could easily argue that it is not necessary to spend a large amount to money to boost the rate by a few percentage points. That choice needs to be made with the awareness that there is no response rate as good as 100%. Anything less is already a compromise and will have an effect on the quality of the data.

7

Where the Data Comes From

Usually studies designed to collect data from citizens focus on the entire community of people served by a recreation agency. However, it is often difficult and unnecessary to collect data from every member of the population. On the other hand, it is possible to carefully select a small number of people and collect information from them and consider that data to represent the entire community. Quite naturally, this means that the small group must be selected carefully so that they indeed are representative of the community. The value of the data, and the recommendations and policy decisions based on the data are only as good as the data, and the quality of the data is severely impacted by the way in which the participants of the study are selected and the way they are asked the questions. The process of sampling ensures that the selection is done in a reliable and valid way.

Generally there are four key aspects to sampling. It is important to consider the definition of the population that will be represented by the sample through a process of randomization that ensures a certain degree of probability that the sample is indeed good. The four italicized terms indicate the four primary concerns in sampling.

Definition of the Population and Listing the Population

In any survey, the first step that needs to be taken is an attempt at precisely defining the population or the community of people whose opinion is sought. In most cases, this group is so large and diverse that it is impossible to ask each members of the group every question. Consequently, it is necessary to select a sample. However, unless it is clear who the population is, it is difficult to decide the method to be used in selecting a representation of the group.

In the case of leisure and recreation surveys, the issue of population definition can often be addressed by thinking of a set of common operational practices of the agency. To begin with, agencies often have to restrict their services within specific geographic areas. For instance, if a city recreation department serves a particular set of zip code areas, then its population of interest in most cases would be restricted to the set of zip code areas. Sending a questionnaire outside of the geographic area of service could be considered an inappropriate use of study resources since the needs, attitudes, and opinions of the people outside the service area are of little relevance to the study.

A second criterion of defining the population is usage. If the objective of the survey is to obtain specialized information about the patterns of use of particular facilities or attitudes and opinions toward programs from people who have already participated in the program, then the population can be defined as users and participators. This definition eliminates from the population those who do not use the particular facility. Such a definition of the population is also tied to the way in which usage is defined. The agency has to consider that question carefully before determining how the population ought to be defined. In most attitude and interest surveys conducted for the purpose of evaluating the existing programs or for assessing future needs, the population is defined as every member in the geographic areas being served by the agency. Distinctions between users and non-users are often made post-hoc, after the data has been collected and some standard usage definition has been established. In many communities, the users are far fewer than the non-users, and a master plan made only on the basis of the responses from users could be politically inappropriate since the non-users' opinions are equally as important where the entire community is concerned.

In some cases, the definition of the population is also tied to age. It is possible that the agency is interested in a particular age group and would want to know its opinions and attitudes. Given the fact that in the twenty-first century there is an increasing number of older citizens in America, it is possible that agencies are interested in knowing more about the needs, attitudes, and interests of these people. In such cases, the agency has to clearly define the age categories so that the particular population can be targeted.

In general, most needs and evaluation surveys connected with planning and development tend to be interested in the general population of the community being served. Since the tax base for most agencies comes from the residents of their recreation districts, it is only right that every member of the community be given an opportunity to provide feedback to the agency.

Once the population has been defined, it is necessary then to obtain a listing of the entire group so that it is possible to select from the group. If the agency conducting the study chooses to do its own sampling, then it is important to recognize some of the common problems associated with population lists.[1]

Although there is increasing availability of electronic databases that list large populations, it is still difficult to obtain listings that are reliable and clean. The key questions that need to be asked of any list are listed here.

Are There any Duplicates in the List?

Very often population lists contain duplicates. A person's address can be listed twice under two different spellings of the last name, or a phone number could be listed twice, once under business and then under the residential pages. Similarly, lists can be compiled from other existing lists leading to duplication because one person can belong to multiple lists and thus appear more than once in the master list. The fact that a name that appears more than once gives that name a higher chance of being selected, violating the randomness of the sample as explained later in the chapter. This can be avoided by looking for and eliminating duplicates. With the increasing use of electronic databases, it is now possible to do that more efficiently.

Are There Omissions From the List?

In many cases, lists are incomplete. Sometimes, due to the timing when the list was compiled, some members of the community will not appear in the list. For example, a phone book published in October of any given year will not contain the names, addresses, or phone numbers of the people who moved into the community in November, and their names will only be included after a year. That is a type of omission where the name or address simply does not appear due to a systematic phenomenon. In other cases, there might be random omissions without any particular patterns. That is less troublesome, since such random mistakes tend to "wash out" when a random sample is selected. However, an agency needs to be attentive to the fact that there are no systematic omissions in the lists. If such omissions are discovered, it is necessary to correct them. Just as duplication leads to the higher chance of the name falling into a sample, omissions lead to a nil chance of the member being included in the sample because the name simply does not appear.[2]

Are There Ineligible Members in the List?

This concerns situations where the population list contains names and addresses that are ineligible by the definition of the population. This happens often in leisure and recreation studies, because there is incongruence between the way the agency might define its population and the way the listing agency would define the population. In one study, for instance, the population was defined by the area that the agency serves. However, the area was not contained within well-defined zip code areas, or a city name. Consequently, zip codes contained part eligible and part ineligible populations. When the sample was selected, there was a portion that was ineligible, and it was impossible to determine who was eligible without time-consuming procedures of matching street addresses with street maps. In such cases, it is best to mail to both eligible and ineligibles (unless the split is 50-50, in which cases attempts at cleaning the list ought to be made prior to excessive mailing to ineligible populations), and then provide ask a question in the questionnaire about the location of the respondent to try and eliminate the ineligible responses from the data set.

Is the List Accurate in its Information?

Sometimes, in spite of best efforts, lists contain inaccurate information. While both omissions and duplication are forms of inaccuracy, there are other miscellaneous kinds of inaccuracies that need to be attended to. Sometimes lists might have wrong addresses and telephone number information. In such case, samples selected based on such inaccurate lists would have mistakes that become inexpensive later in the survey. Two examples should illustrate such problems. In one case, a listing of all white page phone numbers in the United States was obtained from a vendor. Delivered on CD-ROM discs the lists were searchable by a variety of fields including zip+4, city name, phone area code and so forth. It was, however, discovered that in many cases, small cities simply did not appear in the listing. Often the phone numbers of the small cities would appear, but the city name referred to the closest large metropolitan area. In such cases, a geographically targeted sample selected on the basis of a village name would be quite inaccurate. In another case, a vendor provided a sample based on a list that they maintained. While such lists usually have a 98% deliverable rate (i.e., the postal service will be able to find an accurate address in 98% of the cases) this sample provide a deliverable rate of only about 90%. This discrepancy was explained by the fact that the city consisted of areas where the mobility rate was high. Thus, there might be an apartment house where the primary residents are students from a neighboring university. Every fall, there are different people staying at the addresses, and thus while there was a physical address to deliver to, the person listed as the recipient is unavailable. In such cases, simply addressing the envelope with a name along with "or present resident" would have corrected for the problem. Since such situations exist, it is useful for the recreation agency to explore where such problems can occur and plan ahead for that, and not be surprised when an unforeseen problem does arise.

Obtaining Representativeness in the Sample

Once the population has been defined, it is necessary to formulate a method by which a sample can be selected that represents the population. Representativeness involves a process by which all the constituencies in the population have a known chance of being in the sample. For instance, if the leisure agency services a community where 70% of the population is composed of Caucasians and 25% of the population is composed of other races, then these proportions must also be represented in the sample. Consequently, the sampling procedure needs to ensure that the sample contains the same proportions as the ethnic groups. The same is true for other demographic criteria such as gender, age, income level, and household structure. The decennial census is often considered the best estimate of the demographic composition of any population. Consequently, the test of representativeness lies in comparing the results of the study with the census information to ascertain that the results are indeed representative and that the over- or under-representation of any particular group has introduced no systematic bias. However, that determination can only be done after the survey data has been collected when it is too late to correct for any problems with the sampling procedure.[3] Assuming that the sample is representative of the population and there are no specific biases in the sampling procedure, it can be assumed that the sample will also represent the recreation-related attitudes, opinions, and needs of the population. Because recreation interests are often closely linked to demographic attributes, it is quite likely that different leisure interests would be addressed if it is possible to obtain a representative sample from the demographic perspective.

The notion of representation is closely tied to the concept of probability. In a representative sample, it is assumed that every member of the population, independent of his or her demographic category, had an equal chance of falling into the sample. Most often, the process of using a random selection process accomplishes this. By this procedure, every member has a known and equal probability of being included in the sample, and since this probability is known, it is possible to compute the population characteristics from the sample data with the assumption that there were no known biases that gave any particular group a better (or worse) chance of falling into the sample.

Unless the sample is moderately representative, it is not possible to make predictions about the general population from which the sample is selected. Needless to say, a sample can never be exactly representative of the population. However, a random sample selected from the population is often the best means of ensuring representativeness of the community, as compared to samples selected in specific recreation facilities or public areas. For instance, if the population is defined as the people of the community, and the sampling procedure involves selecting everyone who attends the swimming pool activities, the sample represents the users of pools and not the entire population. Consequently, any decisions made on the basis of such a sample will not be generalizable to the population, and plans made on the basis of such data would be flawed and biased. Thus, the notion of randomization and random selection becomes critical to the sampling process.

Random Selection

By definition, a random sample is one where every member of the population has a known and equal probability of selection. Specific steps are needed to make the sample random and to ensure that every member of the population has a chance of being selected in the sample. It is also important to note that the data collected from the sample is indeed an estimate and is never an exact accounting of the population description because it is impossible to obtain the exact population description without collecting data from every member of the population. As a result, the data obtained from the random sample has a margin of error that influences the size of the random sample. Since the sample is a randomly selected sub-group of the population, it is not expected to be an exact mirror of the population. It is expected that the sample would represent the population to a large degree, but it would be an estimate that will differ from the true population measures by a specific amount. Indeed, the quality of the sample is often determined by the extent to which the sample can mimic the population. This is measured as sampling error, which reports the extent of error or "doubt" associated with the sample measurements.

When a population is large, it is theoretically possible to select multiple random samples from the population. Consider, for instance, a situation where the service area for a recreation agency consists of 100,000 people. It is possible to select 100 different samples from this population, each consisting of 1,000 members who are selected without repetition. Continuing with this hypothetical situation, let us now consider that the proportion of men and women is calculated from each of these samples. It is likely that the first sample has 51% men and 49% women, the second sample has 54% men and 46% women, and the third sample contains 48% men and 52% women. The question that the researcher or the agency administrator needs to consider is: Which of these estimates is correct? The answer really is that all of these are correct. These are accurate estimates of the population characteristics. Notice that the percentage of males varies between 54% and 48%. The mid-point of these percentages is 51%, and it is possible to claim that the percentage of men in the population varies between 54% and 48% as well as say that the percentage of men in community is 51% plus/minus 3%. The 3% represents the amount of error associated with the sample and the probability that the estimates of population computed from the sample are within a certain degree of confidence, which is in this case in 95% or above. Since it is impractical to select multiple samples, mathematical procedures calculate the error associated with the sampling process. This error is called the sampling error related to the measurement.

The extent of sampling error becomes the best gauge of the quality of the sample. The lower the sampling error the better the sample, because the sample estimates come closer to the true population values. The sampling error depends on a variety of interrelated factors; however, two qualities of the sample help to reduce the sampling error. Generally, the larger the sample, the lower the sampling error. When the sample and the population are identical, the issue of sampling error disappears because the measurements represent the entire population. However, the relationship between sampling error and sample size is not strictly linear. Increasing the sample size will not necessarily see a corresponding reduction of sampling error. It is a non-linear relationship, one where the sampling error is large with very small samples, but after a particular sample size, the change in sampling error is small even with significant increases in sample size.[4] Consequently, it is important to retain the balance between the sampling error and the sample size, because a larger sample size also always results in a more expensive study. The sampling error has to be maintained between 3% to 5%, suggesting that it needs to be less than 5%, but the sample does not have to be so large that the error needs to be below 3%.

Sample Selection

Most leisure and recreation evaluations use a simple random sample. As discussed earlier, the fundamental assumption behind this sample is that every member of the population has the same probability of being selected and that probability is simply the ratio of the sample size and the population size. In other words, if the leisure and recreation agency services a community of 100,000 people, then a simple random sample of 1,000 would suggest that every member of the population had a 1 in 10 chance of being selected. Moreover, given the assumptions of randomness, the 10% chance of falling into the sample is independent of any pre-existing conditions such as ethnicity, the amount of use of leisure services, and other such demographic or behavioral characteristics.

The simple random sample is best used in leisure and recreation surveys that are attempting to collect aggregate information about the community. Most often, master plans and other long-range planning activities need the input of the general population independent of special leisure needs and interests. In such cases where averages of opinions, interests, and needs are required, the simple random sample becomes most appropriate. It is not the best kind of sampling technique when specific comparisons are to be made between different sections of the population. That is, however, not a common need for leisure and recreation administrators. When the leisure agency is interested in the opinions of the general community, it is not necessarily interested in statistically comparing the differences of need between demographic categories. What is more important is obtaining a representation of the different ethnic and other demographic categories so that the administrators can support their results as representative of the community they are serving. Thus, if the community of 100,000 consists of

7,000 African-Americans, then the simple random sample of 1,000 ought to contain at least 70 African-American members to represent that proportion of the community. In many cases, the simple random sample also proves to be least expensive of all of the sampling procedures because the selection process does not call for any complex manipulation of the population list and thus takes lesser time as well. Finally, the simple random sample can be used in almost any kind of data-collection strategy. There are no specific sampling assumptions that require particular data-collection methods. The simple random sample can be used to produce a sub-group that is amenable to all of the various data-collection technologies.

The process of selection of the simple random sample can be divided into two parts. First, the simple random sample needs a clean and complete population list that is free of the problems discussed earlier in this chapter. Most of these lists are available in digital formats as an electronic file. The file can then be processed with a spreadsheet or statistical program to select a random sub-group from the list.

Alternatives to Simple Random Sample

While the simple random sample serves most of the needs of representativeness, randomness, and the other criteria of sampling, there are occasions when the sampling needs are different from obtaining an aggregate representation of the population. In many cases, the study design could call for objectives that are much more specific where the leisure services administrator needs to have detailed information about specific constituencies whose needs could be particularly different from the overall average needs of the community. In such cases, alternative sampling techniques are required to ensure that the specific study needs are met. Often, the simple random sample becomes inadequate in meeting such needs. The following examples illustrate some of these alternative needs:

- An administrator might need to find out if there are differences between the leisure needs of a particular minority community and the majority of the community he or she serves.
- An administrator might need to know the specific needs of a particular neighborhood within the community he or she serves.
- An administrator might need to know the needs of a section of the community that is rare, such as people with disabilities.

All of these needs call for different kinds of sample designs, and often the specific design precludes the possibility of getting general information about the community. In other words, a sample design that would elicit information about the differences between different sections of the community would not necessarily yield any information about the overall needs of the entire community. However, it is now possible to turn to the three kinds of sample design that would accomplish the above tasks.

Stratification. The process of stratification involves dividing the population into specific groups and then using the categorization as the beginning point for the sampling process. The sampling process itself could be a random sampling within each category or strata or a more complex sampling procedure within the strata. The resulting stratified sample is one that helps to determine the difference between groups. In most measures of difference, a fundamental assumption is that the sample sizes of each of the groups are comparable, so to test for statistically significant differences between groups it is important that the number of people from each group be equal or close to being equal. In the case of a simple random sample, that is simply not the case. As shown in the earlier example, in the case of a sample of 1,000 from a community of 100,000 with 7% minority, only 70 of the 1,000 members would be the minority. In that situation, it might be possible to gain an estimate of the needs of the minority community, but it would be impossible to arrive at specific issues of difference between the minority and the majority.

This calls for stratified sampling where the population is divided into the specific strata of interest and equal-sized samples are selected from each stratum. For example, in the above example, if the interest is in looking at statistically significant differences between the minority and the majority, then there ought to be 500 members selected from the minority and 500 from the majority to accomplish any comparison tasks. This would reduce the error associated with the estimate of the difference and thus provide a correct estimate of the difference between the groups. What is lost in this scheme, though, is the ability to obtain any aggregate results on the total community. In order to make the sample sizes equal, the probability of selection of a member of the minority is radically increased to 500/7,000 while the probability of selection of the member of the majority is sharply reduced to 500/93,000 leading to an over-representation of the minority and an under-representation of the majority. Consequently, any estimates of the total based on this sample would be incorrect.

This is precisely why it is extremely important to determine the goals of the research prior to selecting the sample. Due to the rigors of the needs of statistics, it is sometimes impossible to obtain two goals from the same sample. Comparison between disproportionate groups becomes extremely difficult when a simple random sample is selected, while obtaining estimates of totals are often difficult to obtain when selecting a stratified sample. The selection of the stratified sample also requires some prior knowledge of the population. For instance, in trying to select a stratified sample of minority and majority members of the community, it is important to be able to identify who the minorities are in the population, put them in a different list, and then select equal samples from the two lists.

Cluster sampling. The primary goal of this kind of sampling is to identify specific groups of similar people. For instance, if the administrator of the leisure and recreation department is interested in obtaining the opinion of the youth, it is possible to do a simple random sample, and depending on the nature of the community, obtain the necessary sample size to get a representative size of youth respondents. For example, if 10% of a community's population is between the ages of 11 and 18, and the administrator wants a sample size of 1,000, the agency would have to mail 10,000 surveys or make 10,000 phone calls to obtain the 1,000 youth respondents. This situation calls for cluster sampling.

In the case of cluster sampling, it is assumed that there are geographic areas or other such clusters where the probability of finding people of the kind you are seeking is increased. Most metropolitan areas have specific neighborhoods that are predominantly populated by specific minority groups. For example, if the administrator of Dallas Parks and Recreation Department is seeking to inquire about the needs of the Asian community there, it might be possible to identify neighborhoods where there is a large percentage of Asians and select a simple random sample within that neighborhood. The danger associated with such a plan is that it is possible that there are other Asians in other parts of the city who would be missed by this sampling procedure. While that is a loss, the trade off lies in the fact that the cluster sampling makes it possible to reach people who would otherwise be almost impossible to identify. In the case of the example of the youth, the clusters are schools in the community. These are places where the children and youth gather and they become ideal clusters to sample from.

In the case of selecting a cluster sample, it is important to recognize that this is a two-step process. In the first stage, it is important to select the clusters of interest. This is followed by the sample selected from within the cluster. An important measure associated with cluster samples is the measure of homogeneity within the cluster. Given the assumptions of clustering, it is expected that this would be relatively high to indicate that the objectives of clustering were indeed fulfilled. This has become an increasingly popular strategy in leisure and recreation surveys when the opinion of the youth is sought and schools are used as clusters where the population can be reached.

Network sampling. Sometimes leisure and recreation decision makers need to gather information about specific kinds of populations who are rare and hard to reach. With the increasing concern over the opportunities available to the disabled and with the aggressive adaptation of the American Disabilities Act, there is a need to find out what the disabled have to say about leisure and recreation needs and opportunities. However, this is a rare and often difficult population to reach. In a recent study, only 7% of the respondents indicated that they were disabled, bringing the sample size up to 35 in a sample of 500. Needless to say, there might be more than 35 people with disabilities in the city, and the simple random sample cannot yield all the respondents. In this case, the option of clustering is also absent (unless there are specific and limited number of services where most of the members of the population would go to). However, this is an ideal situation for attempting a network sampling.

In the case of network sampling (often also called "snowball" sampling), a few of the members of the rare population are first identified and then they are probed to see if they know of other people with similar characteristics. Thus, it is likely that one disabled person might know of others in the community and thus a network can be established by which a much larger number of members of the particular community can be reached. This strategy can be used with ethnic groups, special interest groups, and any sub-groups of the community who would have a high probability of knowing others with similar interests (e.g., hobby groups, special sports groups and so forth).

The final concern in any kind of sampling is to settle on a sample size. This is perhaps the thorniest of all the questions that are faced by any person or agency attempting to do a survey. The next section provides some light on the question of sample size.

Determining the Optimum Sample Size

In addition to maintaining the randomness of the sample, making sure that the sample is representative, and finally deciding on the kind of sample to use, the practitioner has to answer another key question about the sample: how large does the sample have to be? Before answering this question, it is necessary to dispel a myth about sample size. The sample does not need to be a particular percentage of the population. Too often leisure service administrators claim that they have taken a 10% sample of the population. The fallacy of this process becomes clear when the following example is considered. If the population of a community is 100,000, a 10% sample would yield 10,000 members in the sample, which is far more than what is necessary to gain good estimates; on the other hand, if the community size consists of 200 members a 10% sample would yield 20 members, which is grossly inadequate. It is therefore incorrect to think of samples as percentages.

In fact, the starting point of answering the question of sample size lies in the issue of error. As indicated earlier, the practitioner needs to obtain an estimate of the population attitudes and opinions from the sample. Needless to say, if different samples are selected, there will be different estimates obtained. These estimates will differ from each other by certain percentages, and the measure of sampling error is expressed as a function of this percentage. If the samples are too small, then the sampling error will be large. In other words, several samples of 50 members will vary largely in their estimates as compared to several samples of 500 members. It is possible to compute the error size based on the sample size and vice versa, but suffice to say now that the error that is tolerable in social science research is between 5% to 3%. Consequently, the sample size is determined by the amount of acceptable error.

In most cases, a sample size of 500 or more results in errors of 5% or less, and it is advisable that a sample size of 650 often produces small enough errors even for populations that are much larger than the sample size. This number is based on the simplification of a set of very complex computations and assumptions. In brief, to estimate the sample size needed to obtain a 5% error on the estimate of gender, it is possible to claim that a size of 650 is adequate.[5] Sample size is also determined by the resources available to do a study. In ideal conditions, it would be best to obtain responses from all members of a population. However, when considering a community such as a large metropolitan area, it is inadvisable to try to conduct a survey with every member of the community. Consequently, it is necessary to strike a balance between how much resources can be spent to obtain what level of error. The attempt is to minimize error as well as minimize costs. This requires difficult decisions about sample size to be made early in the design process. Sometimes the community is so small that every member can be contacted, and in such cases that should certainly be done. In other cases, there are enough resources to go beyond the bare minimum of 650 and there, too, a bigger sample size should be considered. However, it is inadvisable to do a study with an inadequate sample, because even after considerable expense, the results could be flawed and unreliable.

Promising a predefined number of data points is one common example of flawed sampling that is often used by contractors who are interested in promising findings to the recreation agency without guaranteeing that the findings will be reliable. This process is partly facilitated by recreation agencies that are misled by unscrupulous contractors who advise the agencies that it is possible to do studies that yield a certain predetermined number of completed interviews. It is not unusual to see agencies put language such as "must have 500 completed interviews" in their requests for proposals. Such conditions are produced by incorrect information provided by the contractors who are more interested in getting the contract than actually providing reliable data. The primary problem with attempting to reach such a predetermined number of data points is the lack of any logical support for the quota that is set in the request for proposal or by the contractor. Usually quota sampling does not take into account the issues of sampling error, and an arbitrary number is chosen without any sufficient scientific reason to select the number. Indeed, the rationale is often based on what the contractor is able to accomplish within a study budget and still make a handsome profit even though the data quality is poor and the recreation agency is eventually short changed. The quota sampling process also pays no attention to the response rate. The contractor is only interested in meeting the quota that has been preset. For example, if the quota is set at 500 for a population of 50,000 and the contractor is able to somehow yield that 500 by sending out 10,000 questionnaires by bulk mail, then the quota would certainly be met with a response rate of 5%, which introduces unacceptably high non-response error making the data completely unreliable. Indeed, in some cases, the hapless recreation agency cannot even find a clearly reported response rate in reports produced by contractors who use quota sampling to provide unreliable non-generalizable data. Thus, it is very important to shy away from "research" procedures that promise a pre-determined number of interviews but does not elaborate on the ways in which the sample would be selected and how the response rate would be maximized.

Overall, the sampling process is one of the most important aspects of the process of collecting citizen data that can be generalized to a large population. The reliability of the sampling process reflects on the reliability of the data. The specific sampling process, be it random sampling or stratified sampling, also determines the kinds of statistical procedures that can be applied to the data. For instance, data collected using a stratified sampling process cannot be treated the same way as data collected in a random sampling process. In the case of the stratified sample, the probability of selection of a sample point within a specific strata could be different from the probability of selection within a different strata, making it impossible to simply combine the data from the different strata without providing appropriate statistical adjustments for the different probabilities. Such considerations become less complicated for random samples, where the probability of selection remains the same for every data point. This is also the most popular form of correctly done scientific sampling. The next chapter discusses some of the key analytic procedures that can be applied to data collected through a random sampling process.

Notes

[1]Increasingly agencies are turning over the survey process to trained professional organizations such as Management Learning Laboratories, who have the right mix of talents to conduct an efficient survey. In such cases, the professional agency or its subcontractor could be responsible for the sample selection process. In any event, the agency personnel need to be aware of the issues associated with the selection process.

[2]In the mail surveys conducted to assess the attitudes and interests related to recreation and leisure, the population lists are often obtained from utility agencies, departments of motor vehicles, and such agencies who are relatively rigorous about maintaining complete lists leading to little problems with omissions. If, however, the phone book is substituted for the lists, then an immediate problem of omission opens up because the book is dated and increasingly number of people are making their numbers "unlisted," thus voluntarily omitting themselves from the lists.

[3]In some cases, when there is a lack of representation, a mathematics procedure of weighting the results can be done. Simply put, this involves giving a higher weight to the underrepresented constituency and a lower weight to the overrepresented groups. In general, statisticians are suspicious of this procedure when it is used to correct for data-collection problems. It is, however, a necessary procedure in some sampling situations such as stratified sampling.

[4]This will be discussed in greater depth later in this chapter, but suffice to say this relation between sampling error and sample size makes it unrealistic to go for specific percentages of the population because a higher percentage does not necessarily mean a significantly lowered sampling error.

[5]The sample size can be measured using the following formula: sampling error = square root of $[(p)(1-p)/(\text{sample size})]$ where p is the probability that a condition exists. For instance, if the condition is smoking, then p could be 30%, indicating that 30% of the population smoke. In most cases, since the actual value of p is not known, it is assumed to be 50%.

8

Data Analysis

Once the data collection has been completed, it is possible to move on to the next stage of the process—data analysis. The term data analysis can conjure up a variety of images, from those of basic counting of information to very complex manipulation of the data to investigate trends and analyze relationships. The key is, however, being clear about the specific needs of the agency and the reason why the data collection was even attempted. Most of the time, the two broad goals of the data-collection effort are to assess the future needs of the community and to evaluate the current opinion and levels of satisfaction of the community. Based on these goals, the agency should be able to make a set of informed decisions and move on with the process of creating a master plan, strengthening areas of weakness or developing areas where a need is growing. It is therefore important to keep in mind that the process of collecting citizen data is a pragmatic affair with particular actions that need to be taken at the end to make the effort worthwhile. This is not a process of abstract research to find out about the opinions of the population and then conduct elaborate statistical manipulations to test the relationships, differences, and other trends in the data to produce academic papers. On the other hand, the process of data collection is driven by the need to answer specific questions that would allow the agency to do a better job of providing an important service to the community. The data analysis is therefore dependent on the pragmatic needs of the agency.

The process of data collection is taken on to meet a specific set of needs such as:

- Investigate the current level of interest in the specific activities and facilities provided by a recreation provider.

- Investigate what future interests the community might have in terms of specific recreation needs.
- Investigate the opinions of the community with respect to the efficiency and the sufficiency of the leisure services available to the community.
- Gather all relevant demographic and behavioral data that can be used to better understand the composition of the community, its time availability and the way in which time is spent by the community.

The first three of the above require a particular direction of analysis, while the last goal calls for a slight modification of the analysis. However, these goals certainly do not need complex mathematical modeling and other advanced statistical procedures that would simply be irrelevant to the task of fulfilling the goals.

However, before moving on to the kinds of analysis, it is useful and necessary to establish some fundamental notions about the data and the way in which specific attributes are measured.

The Basics

As mentioned in the chapter on questionnaire construction, the final instrument is often a complex product with a variety of questions of different types set up with different kinds of response options ranging from a simple "yes/no" answer to more complicated answer options. Most questions are often constructed as closed-ended questions that offer the respondents a limited set of responses to choose from. In many cases, these options are pre-coded and the data-entry personnel do not have to remember specific code numbers. For instance, if it has been decided that men would be numbered as "1" and women as "2" then those are the codes that would be used consistently throughout the study. The responses on the questionnaires need to be converted to numbers for numerical analysis using computers. The process of conversion is called coding. In some cases, the information is "pre-coded" where the questionnaire would include the number and the person answering the questionnaire would circle a "1" to indicated that the person was a male. In other cases, the word "male" would be circled and that response would be coded as a "1" at the time of data entry. The specific numbers associated with each response are often dependent on the type of scales being used in the questionnaire.

The notion of the scale has major implications on the final data analysis and the way in which it is conducted and the limits and scopes of the analysis. A simple example will illustrate the point. If you want to find out the gender of a person, you ask if he or she is male or female. You might then attach the number "1" to the women and "2" to the men. You can then count how many 1s there are amongst your respondents and how many 2s there are among the respondents. Ultimately, you can claim that there were two hundred 1s and two hundred-fifty 2s among the 500 respondents and 50 people did not answer the question. This means that 44.4% is 1s or women and 55.6% are 2s or men. And that is usually the limit of the analysis. It is meaningless to compute an average and say that the average gender is 1.56, because the number 1.56 is of no value here—gender can be only 1 or 2. However, the situation is quite different in the case of questions where the response can be on a continuum from "strongly agree" to "strongly disagree." Here it is assumed that if the average response is 4.5 where 5 stands for strongly agree and 1 stands for strongly disagree, then it is likely that the average attitude is on the positive side. Moreover, in this case, the policy maker would also gain from knowing what percentage of the respondents said 5, how many said 4, and so forth. What this demonstrates in that different scales have different ways of analysis and provide different opportunities. It is therefore useful to consider the options provided by some of the common scales used in these surveys.

At lowest level are nominal scales. These are scales where the options on the scale simply put names to categories and there is no relationship between the numbers. So for example, in the case of gender, the categories of male and female are mutually exclusive, and giving the number 8 to males and 547 to females would have no impact on the data analysis. In the end, the agency would still be interested in only knowing what percent were 8s and what percent were 547s. The same goes for categories such as race, where the numbers associated with the categories are meaningless and are simply methods of organizing the population into groups. In questions about leisure and recreation needs, questions that deal with specific options fall into this group as well.

This scale thus provides a particular kind of information and does not give the option of conducting some levels of analysis. In the case of these scales, the analysis that can be performed without much difficulty is that of counting. It is certainly possible to count the number of respondents who responded with any of the options in the above question. It is, however, often meaningless to compute averages or conduct other higher level analysis on these scales.

The next level of scales is called the ordinal scale. In this case, the question asks about mutually exclusive categories, but there is a relationship between the numbers. This is not a commonly used scale in leisure and recreation surveys, but it could be useful in asking questions where it might be able to establish some ranking of the respondents. Consequently, it could be useful in cases where the respondents are users and might need to be rank-ordered in some fashion. These scales are useful to see how a respondent might perceive him- or herself in doing a specific recreation activity. For example, it is possible to ask a question where the respondent has to indicate if the individual is an "expert" swimmer or a "novice" swimmer, where the expert is given a numerical value of "5" and the novice receives a "1" and the those in between receive scores of "2," "3," and "4." In this case, it is possible to compute the percentage of respondents who feel they are experts and the percentage for those who judge themselves to have different skill levels. These judgments are based on self-evaluation, and it is impossible to say that the difference between the judgment of "5" and "4" is the same as the difference between the judgment of "1" and "2." In other words, the "distance" between "1" and "2" could be very different from the difference between "3" and "4." This makes it incorrect to compute an average for a scale like this because it is impossible to correctly interpret the meaning of the average number. The inequality between the different points of these scales is critical and is a definitional element of the ordinal scale, where the computation of an average becomes just as difficult as in the case of the nominal scale. Since the numbers are not equidistant on a scale, the average of 2.5 and the average of 1.5 become vastly different, and without a clear notion of the way in which the scale is established, the numbers could be quite meaningless. On the other hand, the computation of frequencies of occurrence is quite appropriate with the ordinal scale.

These problems disappear to a large degree in the case of the third kind of scale, called the interval scale. This is also one of the more popular kinds of scales that one would encounter in leisure and recreation surveys. This scale is also often called a Likert scale after the person who devised it, although a pure Likert scale is far more complex and rigorously produced than the more commonly used version of the scale that is seen in questionnaires. Consequently, it is often better to refer to these as "Likert-type scales" as compared to a true Lickert scale. The most popular example of such a scale is one that places before the respondents a statement and then asks them to express their level of opinion about the statement. Consequently, any Likert-type scale requires two components. There needs to be a statement of action, opinion, hope, interest, need, or anything else that can be stated in the form of a single, clear, and unambiguous statement. Secondly, respondents must be given a limited set of choices to express their level of interest, agreement, liking, etc. with respect to the statement. It is further assumed that the respondent's feeling can be placed on a psychometric scale, where a number, such as 1 could stand for a low opinion, while a higher number such as 5 (in a five-point scale) or 7 (in a seven-point scale) would represent a high opinion. It is also assumed that the difference in opinion expressed by the distance between the numbers 3 and 4' is equal to the difference in opinions expressed by the distance between the numbers 2 and 3. Clearly these assumptions are open for argument. And, indeed, there is a lot of argument about these assumptions. Yet, research and experience have demonstrated that it is possible to obtain accurate and reliable information about people's opinions using such scales.

Consider now, for instance, a single statement followed by the five-point scale that contains a neutral point of 3 in the middle.[1] It is certainly possible to compute the number of people who chose the different responses. Thus, it would be possible to find out what percent of the people responded with "strongly agree," what percent said "disagree," and so forth. However, with this kind of an interval scale, it is also possible to compute an average. So if the mean response is 4, it would provide the basis to claim that the average opinion of the population is on the positive side of the scale. Moreover, since it is possible to compute the mean, it is also possible to compute other higher level statistics such as the standard deviation and tests for statistically significant differences. The interval scale offers computational opportunities that surpass the simpler nominal and ordinal scales. What is lacking in the interval scale, however, is the presence of an absolute zero. In other words, it is very difficult to find measures of attitude where absolute attitudes can be measured. Stop and ask yourself whether there can be a zero attitude that is similar to an empty box where there are zero elements in it. However, there are times when it is necessary and important to measure such zeros or the complete absence of an attribute.

In such cases, the ratio scale is used. This is the same as the interval scale, except that there is a well-defined zero point in the scale. The distances between the various points are equal as in the interval scale and there is the starting point of zero. The point on the scale that has the value 3 is thus defined with respect to the starting point of zero and is thus specifically related with the other points on the scale. Although not used too often in leisure and recreation surveys, one could encounter this scale occasionally.

Moving on from scales, a second important component of any analytical work is the notion of the variable.

Independent and Dependent Variables

A variable is any measurable attribute that can take on different values. For instance, in any population, age becomes a variable element because different members report different ages. On the other hand, there are some attributes that never change, and those would not be considered variables. It is difficult to find such constants in the realm of social science research, but in the natural sciences there are such constants like the speed of light, which is considered to generally remain unchanged. When something does change, it can be labeled as a variable, and there are two principal kinds of variables that any researcher has to consider at the point of data analysis. These are the independent and dependent variables around which many of the analytical questions are asked. An independent variable is the one that the researcher can manipulate in the case of an experiment. In a leisure and recreation survey where there is no manipulation, the independent variable can be interpreted as any variable that can be expected to have an impact on another variable.

The one that is affected by the independent variable is called the dependent variable. Consider a question in the survey that asks the respondent to show his/her level of interest in aerobics. Such questions are often asked on an interval scale and the respondent can indicate great interest (5) to no interest (1). It is then possible to compute the percentages for each response, as well as the mean and standard deviation. However, it can be further argued that it is expected that there could be a difference in the interest based on gender. Thus, men might have lesser interest in aerobics than women might. In that case, the researcher is arguing that gender is an independent variable and the level of interest in aerobics is the dependent variable and there can be further computations conducted to see the relationship between the two. The independent variable often controls the dependent variable and determines the changes in the dependent variables. Very often, a "cause-effect" relationship is assumed between the variables, but in the case of leisure and recreation surveys, it is often enough to establish a relationship between the variable without the existence of a necessary causal relationship. So while it is difficult to claim that gender "causes" a higher level of interest in aerobics, it is certainly valid to claim that there is a statistically significant relationship between the dependent variable of interest in aerobics and the independent variable of the gender.

In the case of leisure and recreation surveys, the standard independent variables are demographics, which includes gender, age, income, race, household characteristics, and place of residence within a recreation service area. Additionally, other issues such as time available for recreation, the reasons for not using public recreation facilitates can be constructed as independent variables that has an impact on the dependent variables. The primary dependent variables are the ones that deal with attitude, interest in current activities, need for future activities and other questions that directly concern the issues of recreation. It is assumed that these issues are dependent on the demographic characteristics of the person. However, in a study, it is often possible to alter the scope of independent and dependent variables. It can often be argued that a particular attitude, for example, the perception of park safety, can have an effect on a behavior (e.g., the number of times one visits parks). In that case, the attitude can be considered to be the independent variable, and the number of times the behavior is performed the dependent variable. The key is the way in which the two variables are related, whenever one variable can be argued to have a "controlling" potential, it can be considered to be the independent variable, and the one that it is "controlling" is the dependent variable. The relationship is, however, much better defined in the case of an experiment where ample care is taken to define the dependent variable well and specific attempts are made to manipulate the independent variable. That opportunity simply does not exist in the case of the survey.

Every question in an instrument is considered a variable. Usually an instrument is designed in such a way that items that are not expected to vary are not included in the questionnaire. For example, in a leisure and survey questionnaire, one would usually not find a question that asks respondents if they are taxed for the use of public recreation facilities. Except in very special circumstances, the answer to the question is not a variable quantity because everyone is taxed, and all the respondents would respond with a "Yes." This is unlike an attitude question that questions respondents' feelings about the quality of recreation they receive for their tax dollars. Needless to say, it is expected that there will be a good amount of variation in that response. Since every question in the survey is a variable, it is possible to use any question as an independent or dependent variable when it is possible to propose a theoretically sound relationship between two or more variables.

Having clarified the different kinds of scales and the notions of the variables, it is now possible to proceed to the different stages of data analysis.

Setting Up the Data for Analysis

The starting point of the data analysis procedure is the returned and completed questionnaire. It is necessary to establish some criteria to determine what is considered a completed questionnaire. As discussed earlier, there can be different ways for making that decision, and the specific researcher or agency can determine that cut off. The next step in the process is the translation of the questionnaire data into a computer readable format. This consists of two stages. First it is necessary to visually inspect the questionnaire to look for obvious problems of questionnaires being completed in a frivolous manner and respondents not paying much attention to the process. If there are lines drawn across questions, frivolous remarks written by questions and there is a general appearance that the questionnaire has not been taken seriously, it is safe to discount the response from the data set. That is, however, not to say that such an act should not be noted, because it might provide good information (although not statistical) about the feelings of one member of the community about the recreation services. Secondly, before proceeding further, it is important to put an identification number on the questionnaire. Unless there is an id number already on the questionnaire, then an ID number needs to be placed on the instrument. Sometimes, after the data entry has been completed, it might be necessary to follow up on a wrong entry. For instance, if in the initial pass of data analysis it is discovered that there is a respondent with the gender 3, which is not a possible response because gender can have only two possibilities, 1, and 2, it signifies a mistake in data entry. In such cases, it is important to return to the original questionnaire and see what the correct response was and make the necessary change. It is impossible to identify that information without access to the identification number.

Some of these stages are now automated with the adoption of Web-based data collection. When a questionnaire is placed on the Web and respondents are able to use a computer to answer the questions, the respondent automatically completes the data-entry process. This eliminates the need for a separate data-entry step and the researcher gains immediate access to the data, making it possible to move on to the different stages of data analysis.

Independent of how the data is entered—from paper or on the Web—there are some common considerations related to the data-entry design. It is presumed that the data entered is numeric data that is eventually available in a digital format that has the following characteristics:

- Every variable needs to have separate column. In cases where the variable needs more than one column, the necessary number of columns must be reserved for it.
- Every questionnaire, identified by the identification number, needs to have a separate row. In cases where there are several questions, it is possible that one questionnaire will take more than one row, in which case every variable is identified by its row as well as column.
- There should be no empty spaces in the file. All missing information should be coded in a predetermined manner.

If these principles were followed, then a "flat file" or a matrix of numbers would be produced, which will have a standardized format. Such a file is made up of a series of numbers where every questionnaire occupies a fixed set of lines with the first few digits representing the identification number of the questionnaire. For instance, if a data set has one line for each returned questionnaire, then columns 1 to 4 are reserved for the identification number. The fifth column of the line is reserved for the first variable that is the first question in the instrument and the columns continue to the last question in the questionnaire. Say a questionnaire has 35 questions, and 200 people completed the questionnaire; the final file would have 39 columns and 200 rows. This is the kind of file that must be produced by the computer program that could be used to create a Web-based questionnaire. It is important to note that some of the programs that are used to do Web-based studies also come with the option to do the statistical analysis. Generally, the kind of analysis offered by these programs lacks the level of sophistication that is needed to get the most amount of information from the data. As such, even with electronic methods of data collection, it is important to obtain the matrix of numbers so that it is possible to export the matrix to computer programs that are designed to do statistical analysis. Once the data file is available, it is possible to move on to the next phase of the actual data analysis, which usually requires the use of a computer program such as CompuRec that can do statistical computations and provide answers that are easy to interpret (see Appendix I for more information).

In general, analysis can have two goals, (1) the exploratory goal, and (2) functional goal. These two goals also occur in the order presented. The first goal of analysis is to explore the data. In this stage, every question in the data set is individually analyzed to discover the various trends in the data. This is a necessary phase that has to be conducted before any further analysis can be performed. The next stage involves the functional goal, where the analyst is interested in getting answers to specific questions from the data. At this stage, the analyst already knows the trends in the data but is now interested in exploring the answers to specific questions. For instance, the exploratory phase might have indicated that 75% of the respondents were interested in swimming, but in the functional phase, the coordinator of the swimming programs might be interested in knowing whether the interest is among the youth or the adults of the community. This "functional" question can be answered by cross-referencing the swimming question with specific demographic questions. The first exploratory step is to describe the data.

Descriptive Analysis

The most fundamental level of description involves how many people responded with a specific response option. The best example of a count is the decennial census. Every ten years, the Census Bureau engages in the daunting task of compiling a reliable count of the American population. Along with that, the Bureau computes different characteristics of the population, such as gender, race, household income, and other parameters that help to describe the American populace.

In many ways, the leisure and recreation studies also provide similar data. To begin with, the leisure studies contain a set of questions about the demographic characteristics of the respondents. It is thus certainly possible to count the number of men, women, people in different age groups, and people with specific demographic characteristics. Similarly, it is possible to obtain counts of the number of people who had different attitudes. In most standard statistical computation software, this procedure of the count is called computing a "frequency" or rapidity of the occurrence of a particular attribute. This computation has several advantages.

First, this procedure can act as an excellent data-cleaning tool. For instance, it is possible that for the question on gender, a data-entry person accidentally entered the number 3. Since this is not a valid gender number ("Male=2" and "Female=1"), it needs to be corrected. However, to identify the problem, it is first necessary to compute frequencies so that such discrepant entries can be identified and corrected. Secondly, some counts provide valuable information about the respondents, and potential problems can be corrected. For instance, in a leisure and recreation survey, it is customary to send the survey by first-class mail to residents in the community without attention to gender. It is assumed that due to random selection and assignment, any subject related bias would disappear. If, however, the results indicate a particularly high female concentration, then there would be reasons to believe that there was an inadvertent bias in the selection or there was a bias in the response pattern calling for post hoc adjustments such as weighting, which could be needed to correct for under- or over-representation of particular groups.

The second important descriptive measure is the computation of central tendencies. The most common measure of central tendency is the mean or the average, which reports the average score on an interval scale. For example, in the case of an attitude question, the respondents usually choose a number between "1" and "5." In such cases, it is possible to compute a mean of the measure to indicate the overall average attitude of the respondents. The computation of the mean is done using the following formula:

$$\textbf{mean} = \textbf{sum of (measure*n)/Total n}$$

For example, in the following example, the measures vary between 1 and 5, and the *n*s associated with each measure is as follows:

respondent	n	n*measure
1	55	55
2	10	20
3	5	15
4	20	80
5	10	50

The sum of the product of the measure and *n* is 220. The total *n* is 100, and the computed mean is thus 2:2. Following that, it is possible to compute the measure of distribution and the sampling error. In most cases, the computer does this and the numbers need to be used in the correct way. It is important to recognize that the mean is most significant in the case of interval and ratio scales.

One other measure of central tendency is the mode. This indicates the category in which the most number of respondents would fall. In the above example, that would be "1," since 55 out of the 100 respondents responded with a "1." What is noticeable is the fact that the mean is a little higher than the mode, suggesting that while a large number of people have responded with a "1," there is still a significant amount who had opinions that fell at a point higher than "1" on the scale. This issue becomes even more important in the case of measures such as income. If in the same sample, there were 30 people who reported their income to be $35,000 and there were five people who reported it as $10,000, but there were 10 who reported their income to be of $250,000, a little reflection will show that the average income measure would be reasonably high since the higher income respondents would inflate the data. In such cases, both the mean and the mode need to be presented because they in combination describe the income category of the population being considered. A measure similar to the mode is the percentile measure, of which the median is best known.

Sometimes it is not only useful to know the central tendency in terms of the average and most frequent, but it is also important to look at the score of the top 95% or the 50% break point. This also provides some indications of the central tendency in the data and supplements the understanding obtained from the mean and the mode.

What should be clear from this discussion is the fact that it is often necessary to obtain information that can be organized around the centralizing tendencies. So, while the counts are important, it is also necessary to see how the data congeals around single numbers that help to make better sense of the centralizing tendencies of the data. However, these two measures raise a new set of questions of the data. While the frequency provides a preliminary picture of the data, and the mean tends to refine that information, it raises the question about the spread of the data. If, for instance, it is discovered that the average attitude toward golf measures at 4.5 on a five-point scale, suggesting a positive attitude, a question could arise about how spread out the data is. In other words, did the respondents all respond with values that varied between "4" and "5," or did the respondents have greater spread, and the mean is 4.5 because many more people responded with "4s" and "5s"? The answer to this question lies in the measure of variance that estimates the distance of each score from the mean. Variation is measured by the standard deviation, which is based on the mean and the distance of each score from the mean. While the computations are complex, suffice to say that the ultimate value of the standard deviation provides an indication of the spread of the data. Also, based on this standard deviation, several further computations can be done, such as that of the sampling error and the measures of difference.

Having obtained these initial descriptions, it is then possible to move on to delve further into the data and begin to understand trends in the data based on some of the independent variables.

Analysis of Trends

A common question that parks and recreation administrators raise deals with the way in which different sectors of the community react to their services. As indicated earlier, this could be an important question within the functional goals of analysis. Board members are often interested in hearing if a particular planning district is in need of a swimming pool or if the elderly feel that there are inadequate recreation opportunities for them. The analysis described up to now does not answer such questions. The descriptive analysis provides the overall aggregate picture without attention to the details of the data, although there is the potential to this analysis. The aggregate picture becomes a good starting point to ask the questions about the ways in which different parts of the population might have varying interests. These questions can arise in two different ways.

First, the planners, administrators, and the board might raise these questions. Thus, there could be specific planning and programming-related questions that need answers based on citizen data. This applies most in the case of development of master plans and long-term planning where the agency might be considering capital investments in the form of new facilities. In such cases, the needs of every constituency must be attended to. Thus, if there is a need for a teen recreation center, then there is a need to know which area would most benefit from such an addition. Similarly if there are particular deficiencies, for instance, in the area of age-specific programming, then it is important to be able to "break" the data into smaller parts and look at each part to see the way in which differences emerge.

Secondly, the data itself often suggests that there might be differences when none were expected. If the data for any particular measure shows a large spread, or standard deviation, it suggests that there was a large range of opinions about the issue. Such situations beg the question about the way in which the data is spread, who has responded how, and why. On the other hand, there are conditions where the standard deviation is so low that there is no reason to expect any differences. For instance, typically for agencies that provide 4th of July activities in America, there is little variance in the question about the interest in such activities. By and large, most respondents show a large degree of interest in such activities. Consequently, doing any trends analysis on such questions is of little value.

The analysis of trends can be conducted in two different ways. First, it is possible to look at the varying responses at the level of frequencies and see how different groups reacted to a question. This is called a cross tabulation analysis, where it is possible to cross-tabulate by age, income, or even another attitude question. Thus, it is possible to ask the question: How many people felt strongly positive toward aerobics as well as volleyball? This could be answered by conducting a cross tabulation of these two variables. Most computer packages offer standard cross tabulation options. Usually the tables are constructed in a way in which the independent variable (such as gender) appears as columns and the dependent variables appear as rows.

A second similar measure would be an attempt to compare the means of different groups. In most statistical computation programs, this process is done with what is often called a "crossbreak." The procedure involves dividing the raw data into different groups, and then computing the mean for each group. In such cases, it is possible to compute the mean for each gender and report the two means. This provides a more detailed picture than the overall number, which does not draw the necessary distinction.

Having done these analyses, it then becomes necessary to move to a greater level of complexity in studying the data. As suggested in the analysis of crossbreaks and cross tabulations, it is possible to describe the ways in which different sub-groups of the data react to specific questions in the questionnaire. However, the question that needs to be raised is: Are these differences due to chance or due to a real difference between the groups? For instance, if the mean attitude toward aerobics among men is 2.4 and among women is 4.5, there is certainly a difference, but it cannot be established simply by examining the two means whether the difference is due to the fact that men and women indeed have different opinions or whether the difference is merely due to chance. Moreover, the other question that needs to be raised is: Is the difference only among the sample of respondents, or would this difference be seen in the case of the population as well? It might be the case that among the sample there was a difference, but when extended over the population, the difference simply disappears. These questions are connected with the notion of statistical significance. Observing a difference is not usually considered enough to make claims about groups. Further tests of the data need to be conducted to establish that these differences are indeed statistically significant within certain acceptable margins of error.

The usual margin of error in the case of leisure and recreation surveys as well as other opinion and behavior surveys is 5%. In other words, the researcher needs to be confident that there is only a 5% probability that the observed difference between the groups is due to chance, but there is a 95% probability that the difference is indeed due to the different attributes of the groups. This number, 5%, is often called the level of significance and expressed not necessarily as a percentage but as "0.05" and is often also given the abbreviation "p." Most social science research requires that the "p" value be 0.05 or less for a data to be considered statistically significantly different.

It is now possible to turn to some of the specific tests of difference that can be performed and the exact circumstances under which they ought to be performed.

Tests of Difference

There are several different measures for testing statistical differences. However, in most cases, the measurements can be determined in the following ways:

- Measurement of difference in count between two or more groups
- Measurement of difference in mean attitude and opinion between two groups
- Measurement of difference in mean attitude and opinion among three or more groups

Each of these measurements calls for the computation of different kinds of statistics. In the case where the differences in count between groups are being measured, the appropriate statistic to use is called the Chi-Squared statistic. The principle behind the Chi-Squared statistic is simply the assumption that there is an expected frequency/count for any item. For example, when comparing the difference between men and women with respect to a activity, if gender played no role, the expected number of men interested in the activity ought to be the same as women. For example, if the question is: Are you interested in aerobics? And the responses are "Yes/No," the corresponding cross tabulation by gender would produce four cells: Men saying "Yes," women saying "Yes," men saying "No," and women sating "No." Additionally, the expected frequency with a sample of 100 would be 25 in each cell. However, in reality, that would not be the case. The Chi-squared statistic thus measures the difference in the expected and the observed frequency and the value of the measurement indicates if the difference is based on gender or just chance.

The difference between two means is measured by the t-test. Here, too, there is an assumption about the expected average, and the observed mean and appropriate statistics are computed to determine if the difference is based on chance or due to a specific attribute such as gender. There are, however, some additional complexities to the t-test.

First, there are sets of assumptions about the variance of the two groups that are being compared. It is assumed in a standard t-test that the variance or the standard deviations of the two groups are comparable. In other words, if all the men in the aerobics example had the exact same response, while the women had responses that varied substantially around the mean, then a comparison between the men and women could be flawed. On the other hand, if the variation is comparable, then a t-test can be performed. There are ways of getting around this problem by doing higher level and modified t-tests where the assumption of equality of variance can be avoided.

Secondly, t-tests can be used for the comparison between two different time frames for the same group. Consider, for instance, a situation where an agency plans to conduct one needs assessment before the building of a new multiuse recreation center, and then one after the completion of the facility. It could be possible to compare the changes in the attitude of the community by comparing the opinions before and after the building of the facility. Assuming random sampling and comparable variance, a t-test can be performed on the means of the opinions to see if there have been any significant changes in attitude due to the new addition. So, the test can be applied to test changes in the same group as they are tested over time.

While the t-test compares means and makes certain assumptions about the variance, it is possible to do comparisons that take the data analysis to a higher level of abstraction and attempt to compare means as well as variance. The most common of these tests is the One-way Analysis of Variance, often referred to as simply the "one-way" analysis.

In the case of the one-way test, the means of two or more groups are compared along with the comparison of the variance of the groups. Thus, it is more powerful than the t-test, because it offers the opportunity to compare multiple groups. The one-way thus becomes the appropriate test to use if the agency is interested in comparing mean attitude between different income levels or racial groups. Here the t-test would be inadequate because that test is not applicable to multiple groups. This is a critical issue in most tests, because the agency would be very interested in knowing if there is a significant difference in planning districts, and if so, which districts are indeed most different.

The one-way test is also similar to another test called the Analysis of Variance (ANOVA), which computes the difference between groups. However, a more complex test is the Multiple Analysis of Variance (MANOVA). This latter test is used in special situations where the effects of multiple groups need to be studied. An example is a situation where the attitudes toward the construction of a new multiuser recreation center are being analyzed. If it can be argued that attitudes might be controlled by multiple facts, such as the number of children in the household and the income level of the household, then it is important to not only look at the differences based on those grouping criterions, but also on the combined effect of the groups. In such cases, the MANOVA would be the appropriate test to perform with the results indicating which of the variables—number of children or income level—has the main effect, and what the interaction effects of these variables are. Based on these results, it would be possible to make certain claims about the determining factors impacting the issue of attitude. It is important to note that the MANOVA is not often used. It is more of a tool for the experimental researcher geared toward the establishment of cause-effect relationships and testing of hypotheses rather than the tool in the hand of the survey researcher interested in the descriptive task of looking at differences and trends.

Finally, in addition to the task of looking for trends and differences, it is often necessary to establish relationships between different elements of the data that can then shed some light on the possible reasons for particular behavior. This is the realm of correlation and regression analysis.

Analysis of Relationships

While the descriptive analysis speaks about the overall makeup of the data, the trends and cross tabulations point toward possible areas of difference, and the tests of difference establish them to be statistically significant. The question that arises out of the analysis is whether these significant differences show the existence of a relationship that can be statistically established. Furthermore, if the relationship can be established, the next question becomes: Is there a causal relationship between the variables?

The following example illustrates the issue. Most leisure and recreation surveys include a question about the information that the respondents have about the agency activities. Consequently, there could be a statement saying: "I am aware of the department's activities," to which respondents could "strongly agree" to "strongly disagree" on a five-point scale. At the same time, such surveys often have a question about the frequency with which the respondent might attend department activities. It is therefore logical to claim that there could be a relationship between the two. However, that intuitive claim can be measured and certain numerical value assigned to the relationship that indicates the strength of the relationship and the direction of the relationship. This value is called the correlation coefficient and is often abbreviated as "rho," which is a measure of two different attributes —the direction of the relationship and the strength of the relationship. The direction is indicated by the mode of the number rho. If it is a positive value, it indicates a positive relationship, and a negative relationship is indicated by a negative value. The strength of the relationship is indicated by the numeric value of rho. When the computed value of the rho is a positive number, it indicates that the value of one variable increases as the value of the second variable increases indicating a positive relationship. A negative rho value suggests that the value of one variable falls as the value of the second variable increases.

The conclusions about the strength of relationship are primarily based on convention and the needs of the research. In the case of social science research, as with the needs assessments and leisure and recreation surveys, any rho under 0.2 is considered to represent weak to no relationship. Values between 0.2 to 0.4 indicate moderate relationships, those between 0.4 to 0.6 indicate strong relationships, and values over 0.6 can indicate the existence of very strong relationships. It is not very often, however, that rho values of 0.8 or higher are observed. However, in the case of other research, for instance, medical research concerning the use of specific drugs, the relationships need to be defined in a different way because the rigors are different.

It is also important to clarify that correlation measures relationships and their strength and not causality. Thus, while a high rho value can indicate a strong relationship, it is incorrect to make the further judgment that the amount of knowledge about department activities "causes" particular kinds of behavior in attendance of the activities. It is indeed true that there is a relationship, but it is not true to claim that there is a statistical basis to establish causality. To claim causality it is important to establish that the variation in the attendance pattern is explained by the variation in knowledge about activities. This is a fine distinction but a critical one.

The assumption here is that there is a certain degree of variation in attendance patterns. Therefore, there would be a distribution of respondents who vary between infrequent attendance to frequent attendance. The causality question in such a case is stated as: What causes this variance, and is there one or more limited number of variables that can explain the majority of the variance in the attendance pattern? This question is answered by the regression analysis, which not only answers the above question but also provides a mathematical relationship between the variables. Based on the relationship, it is then possible to predict, with some measurable degree of confidence, that if the value of one variable is known, it would be possible to predict the value of the other variable, since the mathematical statement establishes a causal relationship. In the simplest form, the linear regression relationship is expressed as:

$$y = ax + b$$

where x and y are the variable and a and b are constants

Using the previous example of knowledge and attendance would illustrate the above. Let us assume that the knowledge question is asked on a five-point scale, and the attendance question is measured as the number of times you have attended district activities in the past six months. Based on the data, it is then possible to establish a statistically significant relationship that is mathematically expressed as:

attendance = 2*knowledge score + 1

Those who scored a 5 on the knowledge measure are expected to have attended activities about a dozen times in the past six months. It is then possible to ask anyone the knowledge question, and depending on the score, it is then possible to predict, with some degree of accuracy, how many times the person has attended department activities. The degree of accuracy is measured by the regression analysis as well. The computations not only provide the values of a and b in the $y=ax+b$ equation, but also compute a value called "R square," which indicates the percent of the variance in y that can be attributed to x. The R square value is in fact none other than the square of rho. Therefore, if the rho value is "1," it can be argued that there is a perfect relationship and 100% of the variance in y is explained by x, and there is thus the possibility of establishing a causal relationship. However, if the correlation is lower, even if the rho value is 0.9, the R square value goes down to 0.81, suggesting now that only 81% of the variance in y is explained by x, and the remaining 19% need to be explained by a different variable. Thus it should be clear that predictable, cause-effect relationships are indeed difficult to establish, and there is always an element of the unexplained variance in the dependent variable.

This concludes the discussion of most of the data analysis steps that could be and need to be conducted with the survey data. In the next section, some further procedures are described that help to verify the reliability and validity of the questionnaire that has been used in the data analysis.

Factor Analysis and Reliability Checks

When using an instrument, there are sets of assumptions made about the questionnaire that sometimes need to be checked and validated. These assumptions have to do with the notions of the internal validity of the research process, which concerns the procedures used in the conduct of the study. Thus, it is important to be convinced that the questionnaire is indeed measuring what it is supposed to be measuring, and when conclusions are drawn about such measurements, those are reliable and valid conclusions. Additionally, the research needs to be externally valid so that the results of the survey can indeed be generalizable over a larger population. Much of the concerns over sampling and random selection have to do with the issues of generalizability or external validity.

However, returning to the issues of internal validity and reliability, it is important to be able to establish that items in the questionnaire indeed measure the construct that the researcher is trying to get at. For example, if there is an item in the questionnaire that states: "I feel safe in the parks," there is a possibility that respondents could interpret "safety" in terms of violence to themselves, or in terms of the security and maintenance of the park equipment. These are completely different constructs. In the former situation, a recreation department can often do very little to make sure that there are no antisocial elements in the parks, but if safety is related to the maintenance of park equipment, then the department is directly responsible for the safety. However, the department or the agency has no good way of determining how the community is interpreting the statement.

In cases like the above, it is possible to do a reliability check on the instrument. It involves comparing the responses of randomly selected members in the community and then studying the level of agreement between these random members. If there is a large degree of agreement, it can be argued that the community is interpreting the question in the same way, although doubts still linger about the exact interpretation (this is why it is necessary to pay attention to the design and construction of the questionnaire and to conduct focus groups to focus in on what the key issues are).

The best way to do this comparison is to do multiple tests. If the same questionnaire is applied to different samples from the same (or similar) population, then these responses can be compared. However, given the fact that these questionnaires are often specifically designed for the needs of a specific community, there might not be a good history of the use of the questionnaire to draw upon existing reliability data. Concurrently, it is often impractical to try to administer the questionnaire more than once to different samples just to obtain the reliability data. Consequently, a method called "split-half" method is used, where the sample is randomly split into two halves and the responses of the two halves are compared. This provides a good measure of the reliability, and the popular statistic used is called Cronbach's alpha, which can have a value between "1" and "0" where the "1" value represents a highly reliable measure. An alpha value between 0.8 to 0.6 can be considered to be very reliable.

It is important to note that the reliability measure is done after the data has been collected and cannot affect the data-collection procedure. So, if unreliable items are discovered in the questionnaire, the department has to be careful about paying too much attention to those items, because it is simply unclear how good those items are and what they are measuring. Needless to say, if the questionnaire is to be used in the future, those items need to be restated or removed. Finally, some of the doubts can be resolved by post-hoc focus groups, where members of the population are invited back into the group discussions to help interpret some of the data and see how ambiguous items could have been interpreted.

Along with reliability checks, it is also often necessary to conduct analysis that will provide information about the way in which the questionnaire measures broad concepts. Often, particularly with the attitude items in the questionnaire, multiple items attempt to measure the same construct. For example, in one community in the Midwest, there was a great deal of concern about non-residents coming in and using the facilities. The issue was so important that based on the focus group data, it was deemed necessary to include a set of items in the questionnaire that would address the broad notion of "how to handle the non-resident issue." However, what always remains unclear is to the extent to which the respondent interprets that the items deal with the same issue. Even when the items might be clubbed together, there could be situations where the responses might not demonstrate that the items were interpreted in the way intended.

However, a factor analysis, which computes a set of statistics, and then reports different clusters around which items congealed can measure such conceptual clustering. For instance, in a questionnaire with 50 questions, the researcher could have a computer calculate five factors around which the items can be clubbed. At the end of the analysis, the items can be arranged in groups of 10 based on the weight each item had for each factor. If, for example, one item had the weights 0.4, 0.6, 0.2, 0.1, 0.1 for the five factors, it would be assumed that it weighs heavily on the second factor, and should be clubbed with that. The researcher can then observe the five factors and make the decision whether the similar items do indeed cluster around one factor. If they do, then that factor can be called the "non-resident" factor.

Usually there are two outcomes to this analytical approach. First, the researcher might notice that issues unrelated to the "non-resident" problem are also appearing in the factor that has been labeled as the "non-resident" factor. This could call for a finer factor analysis, and instead of five factors, it could be necessary to use seven or eight factors and see how the new clusters look. Secondly, it is possible that an item that the researcher felt was associated with the non-resident issues does not appear in the cluster. This suggests that the way the item was interpreted by the respondents was different from the way it was intended. In such cases, it is instructive to note how the particular item did indeed weigh on what factor. Moreover, in such cases, it is a danger to include that item in any clubbed series. Often to get a bigger picture, items that load on the same factor can be summed together to produce a composite measure that can be used for correlation and other statistical manipulations. In such cases, it is important to be able to determine what indeed are the appropriate scores to club together. In such situations, the factor analysis becomes critical.

Finally, it is important to recognize that both the reliability checks and the factor analysis help to better understand the questionnaire, but they are not descriptive tools that help to make recommendations for the department. These checks help the researcher to understand better how reliable and valid the data is and provide a check on the questionnaire and the data-collection process. Often in the final report this analysis is not reported. The next section will address the question of reporting information collected in the process of the research and how that data can be presented in a way that it is useful to the end user—the agency personnel.

Note

[1]It is important to note that there is a growing tendency among scholars and researchers to abandon the mid-point and use four-point scales, with a different number such a "8" being provided as a "do not know" response. This response is then discounted from the final analysis. However, a counter argument could be made that lack of information or knowledge does not necessarily presuppose a lack of opinion. Thus, to discount the neutral opinion is to force people to have opinions when they might not. Given this, it is important to consider the implications of the even-numbered scales. If one is to be true to Likert, then the five- or seven-point scale is recommended.

9

Managing a Study

The process of collecting citizen input has a series of theoretical components as discussed so far, but there are also significant issues related to the execution of the process that require attention. This chapter focuses on some of the management issues related to collecting data from citizens. These issues need to be considered carefully when deciding on taking on the task of collecting citizen input.

Timing

One of the most important considerations about collecting citizen input is deciding when to actually contact the citizens. There are two types of contact. First, some members of the community are requested to attend focus group meetings. These are meetings where the citizen must come somewhat prepared to discuss issues that would inform the questionnaire construction process. This is not a public meeting where interested people just stroll in for an hour. The focus groups usually involve dedicated people who have sufficient knowledge about their area of specialty to make a contribution to the process. This dedication fortifies the process because the participants usually have a commitment to the community and are willing to take time to come to the meeting even though it could cost them a couple of hours. The focus group meetings also precede the actual data collection and usually would happen about four weeks prior to the time that data collection begins with questionnaires sent to the community. Thus, the key decision about timing relates to the best time to begin data collection by sending the questionnaire to the community.

The decision about timing also needs to be placed within the perspective of the general climate related to general population data collection in the latter part of the first decade of the 21st century. The American population is considered to be over-surveyed. Professional organizations that keep track of the number of questionnaires that an average citizen is expected to complete annually has risen over the years. In general, people have become weary of answering questions that are sent to their homes by mail, arrive in their e-mail inboxes, and are asked by telephone interviewers right as the family is sitting down for dinner.

This excess has made it relatively difficult to obtain the high response rates that are desirable in general population studies. However, a good researcher always attempts to maximize response rate to ensure that the data is of high quality, and one way to damage response rate is to try to conduct data collection when members of the population are least inclined to answer questions. There are two such periods in the United States. One begins with the Thanksgiving holidays and ends after the beginning of the following year. This period of nearly five weeks is not a good time to contact citizens and ask them to answer questions. People are busy with other activities in this holiday period and are not inclined to answer questions. Indeed, bothering them at this time could have a negative impact on the image of the recreation agency because it demonstrates that the agency is insensitive to the demands placed on an average American at that time.

In a similar manner, the other period when an average person is busy is usually related to the school schedule of a region. Families with school-age children are often less inclined to respond to questions in the period immediately following the date when schools shut down for the summer holidays and the period immediately prior to the date when schools reopen at the end of the summer holidays. Traditionally, this has been the "vacation" time for many Americans, and as such, people are usually not available or interested in answering questions. Generally, these periods should not be utilized for data collection, although these times can be used for focus group meetings.

While these are some of the general time periods when data collection could prove to be a challenge, some local timing considerations might also be very important. It is usually not a good idea to attempt data collection at a time when there are other important events going on in the community, such as an election when a new commission might be getting elected. Data collection at such a time could be a distraction. There could also be local issues going on when conducting data collection that might unduly skew the data because of temporary issues that might not have long-term implications but could affect the quality of the data that would be used for long-term planning. These events are difficult to predict, but it becomes the responsibility of the stakeholders involved with the data-collection process to ensure that the data collection is not timed to coincide with events that could have an impact on the quality of the data.

The final consideration about timing relates to the amount of time that it actually takes to do the activities that connect directly with the citizens. Unless there are inordinately large number of focus group meetings, these can usually be completed within four to five days with meetings scheduled all through the day, allowing different kinds of people to attend the meeting. Meetings held early in the morning and those conducted during the typical "lunch hour" are often very convenient for people who work a normal work shift and can use the time before work starts or during lunch to participate in the focus group. Evening hours are always good for most categories of people, whereas youth focus groups are best conducted during the school hours, since these meetings are often done on school premises. The elderly members of the community who come to focus group meetings sometimes prefer early afternoons. However, it is not very difficult to make up a four-day schedule that allows for different time slots and can accommodate about six to seven meetings each day. These meetings need to be completed about a month before the scheduled date for data collection.

The time required for data collection depends on the type of method used for data collection. Generally, it takes the longest to conduct data collection by mail. It is wise to allow at least three full weeks from the date of mailing of the questionnaire to the date that can be used as the end of the data-collection period. Sometimes data continues to come in after the three-week cut off and the researchers must make the decision as to how much of the "late" data would be included in the final data set. Generally, the best option is to include every piece of data that can be included while staying true to the overall time line of the project. Data collection using the Internet is the quickest form of data collection in most cases. Overall, it is important to build in sufficient time for data collection so that this crucial activity does not have to become rushed. The timing of the project and the time allowed for the project both become important components of the management of the data-collection process.

Process and Skill Management

The process of collecting citizen input includes many different steps, each one of which has to happen in an efficient manner to ensure that the final data is high quality. All elements also have to be managed correctly to ensure the smooth operation of the overall process. This means that a recreation agency needs to assign the process to a particular person who would be able to oversee each component of the process to ensure that the process is done in the scientifically correct way. This person might not be the one who actually does the process but is the one who makes arrangements for the process. For instance, a crucial element of the process of data collection is questionnaire design that is initiated with focus groups and use of standardized question banks. The process manager would be the person who makes all the arrangements for the focus group meetings—from inviting the participants to arranging for beverages—but the process manager might not be the one who is actually moderating the meetings. This task requires very special skills related to interpersonal and group communication, and the process manager must find someone to actually run the meetings and gather the information needed to create the questionnaire. The process manager therefore has the responsibility of identifying people inside the recreation agency who can provide the skill sets for the different components of the data-collection process. This is an especially critical task, since it is often the case that the process manager must be able to identify different people who bring different strengths to the process.

The people who are involved with the different components of the process must constantly remain in contact with each other so that all parts of the process are known to all members of the process team. The process manager must ensure that this contact is maintained and there remains a balance between the different parts of the project. For example, the person responsible for designing the questionnaire must be in communication with the person who would eventually do the data analysis. The analyst will have comments about the kinds of analysis that can be done with different kinds of questions, and such discussions should happen before data collection starts to ensure that the overall goals of the project are adequately met. At the same time, the person designing the questionnaire must not have an upper hand in the process, because the loss of balance could easily lead to poor data. The person managing the process must be well aware of the potential problems that could lead to data of poor quality; the ultimate goal of this person should be to ensure that the data is good and reliable.

Resource Management

The data quality is not only dependent on the appropriate timing of the project and the personnel assigned to the project but also on the resources that are assigned to the project. There are many different kinds of resources required for these projects. The most valuable resource is personnel who would be able to dedicate a significant amount of time towards the process. A recreation agency must assume that the person managing the data-collection process would be unavailable for the "regular" work of the person for the duration of the project. These projects require constant attention and the ability to direct other people to do their tasks. As such, the person managing the project must be in a position of authority who can ensure that all the other personnel who are working on the project perform their tasks. It is usually not a good idea to assign the project to a temporary employee or someone who is lower in the organizational chart simply because that person appears to have some extra time. The decision about the person who handles the task must be based on the managerial skills of the person and the amount of authority the person has and not on the fact that the person appears to have some free time. Other people who perform other tasks such as questionnaire design, sampling, data analysis, etc. must also be allowed to take time off from their normal duties to do the tasks that best suit their skill set. During the conduction of the process, the staff of the recreation agency must assume that some of their personnel will have to devote significant amount of time to the process, leading to a domino effect, where others in the staff must fulfill the work of the people who get involved in the project. The process of data collection requires significant time on the part of some staff members, and there must be a plan in place to ensure that there is sufficient personnel resources to do the project and the everyday functions of the agency.

There are some direct costs associated with the process of data collection as well. The recreation agency must set aside funds to pay for standardized banks of questions that can significantly reduce the cost associated with focus groups. Similarly, there are specific costs associated with the purchase of random samples that would represent the community and offer an unbiased data set. These are products that have to be procured from vendors, and the recreation agency would not be able to create these resources internally. On the other hand, the recreation agency might be able to work with the printing services of a county or municipality to print the questionnaires and related material that is used for data collection by mail. The agency might be able to get that activity done "internally" without incurring a large cost. If the data collection is conducted over the Internet, then the agency might be able to work with the department of information services for the programming and hosting of the questionnaire. However, these arrangements must be discussed at the very inception of the process so that the agency can create a realistic budget of the direct costs. In the case of data collection by mail, it is also important to build in the cost of postage for sending out the questionnaire package and the cost of receiving the completed questionnaires back by pre-paid envelopes. The latter cost can only be an estimate.

As should be evident from this discussion, there are significant costs involved in the conduct of a study that yields reliable and usable data. Shortchanging any of the resources results in mistakes that can compromise data quality. Decisions made on the basis of inaccurate data can lead to very costly mistakes in the long term. Also, there is a political cost related to the collection of citizen data. When an agency takes on the responsibility of collecting data from the citizens, they must be able to defend their process so that any potential criticism of the data can be handled swiftly and confidently. Any signs of impropriety in the data-collection process not only damages the quality of the data but can do long-term damage to the image of an agency and its leadership. Consider for instance, a situation where an agency decides to save money and generate its own sample instead of getting the sample from an independent vendor. When that information becomes common knowledge, there could immediately be accusations that the agency has selected the names of the recipients of the questionnaire based on certain criteria known only to the leadership of the recreation agency. This creates a culture of suspicion and only increases incipient distrust of government that is becoming commonplace in America. For many of these reasons, many agencies choose to hire a specialist to do the citizen data collection. The next chapter examines some of the issues related to obtaining outside expertise for this task.

10

Outsourcing

As described in the book thus far, a specific set of steps need to be followed when collecting data from citizens, and each step must be done properly to ensure that a high data quality is eventually obtained. In summary, these steps are made up of: (a) research of existing documents about a community and the available recreation opportunities, (b) focus groups meetings, (c) questionnaire design, (d) statistical sampling, (e) systematic data collection, (f) statistical analysis of the data, and (g) preparation of a specific report with action plans and recommendations. As suggested in the earlier chapter, these tasks require a special set of skills and specific specialized training that include: (a) good communication skills, (b) training in questionnaire design, (c) knowledge of statistics, (d) excellent report writing skills, (e) organizational and project management skills, and (f) computer literacy.

It is the combination of the efficient completion of the tasks using the best of all the skill sets that results in a final report that can be used by the recreation agency to make effective decisions. A gap in the tasks or weakness in any of the skill areas would result in a report that might not be useful and could prove incorrect and thus be detrimental to the decision-making process.

In most cases, a recreation agency does not have all of the required skill sets to complete all the required tasks. In such situations, an agency might begin a process in-house and then realize that the process takes up too much time for inadequate resources and the end result is not very useful. Therefore, if a recreation agency chooses to do a study in-house, it must be able to first ascertain its internal skill sets and make a full and realistic commitment of staff and resources so that all the tasks are properly and correctly completed. As discussed in the earlier chapter, there are significant costs in doing an internal process of collecting citizen data and there is little cost saving to conducting the process in-house since the total cost (including staff salary for the people assigned to the project) can exceed the cost of outsourcing. Sometimes there will be volunteer groups that might come forward to help the agency with the process of collecting citizen data. To be sure, data-collection efforts conducted by volunteers often result in incomplete products and often go over the timeline since by nature the volunteering process assumes a nominal and optional commitment.

It is also important to reiterate the political aspect of the process as discusses briefly earlier. One of the most important characteristic of a proper process of collecting citizen input is the lack of bias. An in-house study, even if done in an objective and careful way, can carry the stigma of bias. It is possible for the citizens to argue that "pre-existing notions" of the recreation agency staff tainted the process, and thus the results can be construed to be a ratification of what the staff "wanted to hear." This allegation can be deflected if the recreation agency can demonstrate that the entire process was turned over to an independent and reputable research laboratory who does not have any "stake" in the outcome of the process. This is an important issue when considering who should be doing the study. It is always better to select a research laboratory that doesn't have a "hidden agenda." For instance, if the outside consultants have a relationship with, or are a part of a planning firm, then there could be a conflict of interest where the results of the data-collection process could reflect certain preferences that might be beneficial to the planning agency's future contracting prospects with the recreation agency. Thus, a planning agency specialized in development of playgrounds might choose to ask more questions about playgrounds and eventually report a high need for playgrounds that the same firm might be hired to develop and construct. For reasons like that, there needs to be a separation between the researchers who are selected to collect information from citizens and other contractors who can stand to benefit from what the data might report.

In the end, turning over the process to reputable researchers helps to reduce a significant amount of worries for the recreation agency and also produces an outcome that the agency can use as unbiased data for further decision-making.

Criteria for Making a Wise Choice

The decision to use researchers to conduct the process does not absolve the agency of all responsibility. The agency leadership must select the appropriate person or group to do the data collection, and the agency must be able to defend its choice. A few basic criteria become important in making this choice: The researchers should be able to claim a lengthy research experience demonstrating expertise in doing research in leisure and recreation needs assessments over a length of time, and the consultants should have skills both in social science research as well as an understanding of the recreation component of the study. Often recreation agencies would contact marketing firms for doing the data collection. However, as is obvious after reading this book, the process of collecting citizen input with respect to recreation and leisure activities requires a unique understanding of recreation practices, and market researchers are not usually equipped with that. On the other hand, recreation planners and people in the industry might have a strong recreation background but would not know much about the process of conducting evaluation and survey research. It is also important that the consultants demonstrate experience in operating at a national level as well as in a cross-section of agencies. Consultants with only local experience working with agencies that are similar to each other does not include the breadth necessary to conduct a complete and comprehensive data collection process. The national experience helps to provide a particular broad perspective to the process and to the results.

Some of the key criteria to look for are (a) experience in both recreation and survey research, (b) experience at the national level, (c) lack of any potential conflict of interests, and (d) long years of experience in specializing only in doing data collection related to recreation and leisure. It is indeed important to seek a research laboratory that would be able to demonstrate all of these qualities rather than just any one or few of them. Indeed, it is usefully to consider some of the common myths and mistakes about the selection process to ensure that a recreation agency does not repeat errors made by other agencies.

First, there is a common tendency to select the firm that would prepare a master plan to do the data collection as well. Unfortunately, it is almost always the case that hiring the same firm to do both the master plan and the data collection from citizens will result in significant conflicts of interest. The planning firm could be more interested in targeted results from the needs assessment that can lead to further business opportunities. Also, planning firms usually do not possess the skill sets required for conducting scientifically valid citizen data collection.

Second, sometimes recreation agencies look for the "single-stop shopping" and find a single firm that can do it all, or a single firm that can patch together several sub-contractors all answering to the principal planning consultant. Although it appears convenient to go to one firm that would then sub-contract the data-collection process to a research laboratory resulting in single-stop shopping for the recreation agency, the associated cost in unnecessary overheads paid to the "primary" firm is usually higher than dealing directly with two primaries, one for the needs assessment and one for the planning component.

Third, recreation agencies sometimes prefer to select a local firm in the same city or region where the recreation agency is located because there is a myth that the local consultant is better than someone from a different area. Yet, as is evident in the description of the process of data collection, and given the availability of numerous tools for communication and research, geographical location of the research laboratory has little relevance to quality of work. Increasingly, location has become relatively redundant, and it is possible to work very efficiently with a research laboratory that could be on the other side of the country. The selection criteria need to be sensitive to the quality of the research laboratory or group and not location.

On the other hand, a fourth belief is that a large market research firm with an international reputation would necessarily be better at doing recreation-related data collection. Unfortunately, large market research firms can appear to be "efficient" with lots of "bells and whistles" in their publicity material and presentations, but such firms are often somewhat generic in nature and claim expertise in divergent contexts of research. Such firms often do not claim expertise in recreation, which remains an important criterion for selecting who to outsource to.

Finally, the most common mistake is to select the group that offers to do a study for the lowest price. Research groups associated with universities and colleges are often those that can offer low costs and reputable researchers. However, before selection a research group based on price, it is important to consider who will actually be doing the different components of the data collection process. For instance, if a university is doing the work, then it is important to know if a survey research center of the university is doing the work. In such cases, there is little cost savings and selecting such a unit is no different from selecting a market generic market research firm, because there are no survey research centers in any American university that can claim specific expertise in doing citizen data collection with respect to recreation and leisure. On the other hand, sometimes a professor who teaches within a department of recreation and leisure would conduct the data-collection process as a class practicum for a research methods class with students doing all the work. Such situations might appear to be less expensive and therefore attractive options, but a recreation agency needs to be very cautious and ensure a strict time line so that the project is completed within the semester or quarter time for which sessions run at the university. If the project is not completed within the time frame, it might take a long time to complete the project until a new class of similar type is offered.

In the end, even in a price-conscious environment, it is not safe to go with the lowest bid without carefully examining why the bid is lower and if there are hidden costs. Sometimes a low bid is a result of inexperience on the part of the consultants, which could eventually result in cost overruns or inefficient research. It is often more important to examine the process being used and then ascertaining the cost for different components of the process.

Steps in Selecting a Research Group

This section examines some of the key steps that are involved in initiating the search for a research group and the process of selecting the appropriate researchers or research group. In most cases, the process involves the creation of a request for proposal (RFP), receiving a set of proposals, and objectively evaluating the proposals. Much of what has been discussed in this book helps to do all of the above.

The process of creating a RFP can be simplified by examining some of the standard language used in previous RFPs. The RFP could be quite standardized with some specific information about any unique issues in the community. Indeed, it should be the job of the proposer to do the necessary background research before preparing the proposal, and it is not necessary for the preparer of the RFP to lay out the background information in too much detail. Indeed, the process of selection becomes simpler and fair if all the proposers are asked to offer the same kind of information in preparing the proposal. Usually, the RFP does not have to be long; a good RFP is precise and to the point. Typically the RFP should have the following sections:

- **Purpose:** This section should describe the goals to be addressed in the study. These goals could be similar to the ones described earlier in this document.
- **Scope of Work:** This section should elaborate on the methodologies desired, sample design, mode of data collection, data processing, analysis, and presentation.
- **Format of Proposal:** This section should describe the format desired for the proposal and it should reflect some of the formatting ideas described in the next section.
- **Submission Method:** This section should describe how the proposal should be submitted, the number of copies desired, and the exact deadline.
- **Evaluation Criteria:** This section should describe the criteria to be used to evaluate the proposal.

At the least, the RFP should specify that the proposal must use a standard format that enumerates the following:

- Overview of the proposer's research firm history, experience and qualifications
- Detailed description of the experiences of the key personnel who would be involved in the study
- Detailed description of the technological and statistical facilities available to the proposer
- Name, address, and phone number of all clients who the proposer has worked for within the previous sixty months
- Detailed description of each step of the methodology with an explanation for why the specific methodology is needed
- Explanation of the way in which the methodology makes optimal use of resources

- A clear delineation of the time required to conduct the study
- Detailed description of the deliverables to be provided at the end of the study
- Detailed description of the computer program that will be provided at the end of study for ongoing analysis of the data
- Evidence of past performance in the form of letters from past clients, news reports of previous studies, etc.
- Evidence of scholarship in the area of recreation needs assessment in the form of publications and other peer reviewed work
- Fixed cost that includes all expenses

All of these points deal with the different and important aspects of the process of doing data collection as discussed in this book and deal with the logistics of the process. Once the eligible proposals are all received, a "blind" process is recommended so that the selection process can be as unbiased as possible. The first way to avoid bias is to include several people on a selection committee. Leaving the selection process only to the director or the higher level administrators of the agency can lead to bias or can be perceived as biased. It is best to include representatives from the staff, citizens, and elected bodies in a selection committee with odd number of members to avoid the "hung jury" condition with even numbered members. The second way to avoid bias is to use a standard set of criteria in the selection process. This set is best conceptualized as a set of questions, and the evaluation process compares the answers to the questions provided in the proposal.

An important question to start with is: How many years of experience does the proposer have? A proposer should be able to claim a lengthy research experience demonstrating that the proposer has been doing research in collecting citizen data with respect to leisure and recreation over a length of time so that it can address some of the trends in recreation and leisure needs and attitudes.

The second question would be: Can the proposer claim expertise in survey/ evaluation research as well as recreation/leisure research? As indicated so far, a combination of skills is required for proper data collection, and only researchers who can perform all the skills should be considered for doing the data collection.

A third question should be: Does the proposer use standard and established research methodologies? There are standard methods for the conduct of focus groups, construction of questionnaires, sampling design, data collection design, statistical data analysis, and data reporting. These methods are laid out in this book and other similar literature regarding citizen data collection. A proposer must be aware of this literature and be able to make specific reference to methodologies in the proposal.

Related to the question on methodology is the next question, which asks: Does the proposer have state-of-the-art technology for data collection and analysis? As is clear from reading this book, there are many different methods of data collection and analysis that have emerged with the explosion of technology. The proposer must be able to demonstrate that it has the technological facilities and the know-how to do the work necessary when attempting to collect reliable data from the general population.

The data-collection process should also not finish with the presentation of a hard-copy report, but the data must be returned to the agency who paid for the collection of the data. However, the data by itself is not very useful unless it comes with a tool that will allow the agency staff to easily analyze the data and add to the data if desired. Thus, the best proposer must also demonstrate that it is able to provide the tools for the recreation agency to continue to mine the data.

As demonstrated in this book, correctly conducted needs data-collection processes require appropriate allocation of limited resources, which leads to the question: Does the proposer show an optimal allocation of resources? For instance, to the reader of this book, it would be clear that a proposal that suggests a huge sample size is not necessarily good, because the funds required for the larger sample size could be allocated to do a follow-up mailing to increase response rate or to increase the number of focus group meetings. Examples such as this suggest that proper allocation of resources is needed to obtain the best result without emphasizing a single component of the research too much.

While all of the criteria and formatting needs help the selection process, what matters in the end is the scientific validity of the data collected. As such, a winning proposal must demonstrate all of the following:

- The proposal should not substitute scientific data collection with community outreach and depend only on community meetings and focus groups. Those methods are necessary to support the comprehensive and scientific data-collection process but cannot substitute a scientifically conducted needs assessment.
- The proposal should demonstrate a clear statistical sampling process that collects data that represents the community at large. Thus, proposals that suggest data collection by "convenient" methods such as distributing questionnaires at community centers and special events or by e-mail need to be treated as non-random designs that will have biases and will not represent the community. Similarly proposals that rely on "quota" sampling should not be trusted.
- The proposal should demonstrate an understanding of the fact that the data-collection process is expected to provide community-level data and not user-level data. Usually the community data includes information about non-users and that information is critical in a comprehensive community-wide needs assessment.

4. The proposal should demonstrate efforts to produce a customized questionnaire for the specific needs assessment without relying on standardized pre-formatted questions and question banks.

The process of preparing a RFP and selecting the research group should be done carefully to ensure high quality of data and to ascertain that the data collection process is conducted in resource-efficient manner. Table 10.1 provides a numeric criteria to evaluate proposals.

Table 10.1
Numeric Criteria to Evaluate Proposals

Quality of method used for development of questionnaire (focus groups, use of reliable banks of questions etc.)	330
Experience with data collection and analysis using the appropriate technology (sample design, mail/Web combination, data analysis plans, etc.)	220
Experience (years of work), academic training (level of education – doctoral degrees, etc.), academic reputation (number of books, publications, research presentations, etc.) of assigned personnel in the area	140
Quality and format of proposal format (simplicity, elegance, etc.)	10

All of these issues are extremely important in making decisions about the way in which the data collection should be conducted to ensure that quality of the data is high. Indeed, as the next chapter demonstrates, there are many different ways of utilizing the data, but the utilization would be worthless if the data collection was done in an incorrect way by researchers who lack the experience and training in doing citizen data collection in the area of recreation and leisure.

11

Data Utilization

The process of collecting citizen data is a very pragmatic process that has specific consequences for the agency. Unlike "basic" research that might be conducted by a researcher at an university, the citizen data-collection process is "applied" research, and the findings from the process must be used in specific ways that would provide the agency with a "return on investment" that has been made to conduct the data-collection process. This return takes many different forms and the agency should be able to maximize the value obtained from the data-collection process. This chapter points towards some of the key outcomes of the process.

Decision Making

One of the ways in which the data becomes meaningful is its role in helping make specific decisions related to the activities of the agency. There are several different layers to the decision making aid. Some of the decisions could be very mundane and would deal with short-term questions. For instance, the data could yield information about specific recreation needs related to specific age groups. That information can be used to make decisions about the way in which specific programs can be promoted to different age groups. The marketing personnel of an agency can decide that some age groups have a greater need for specific kinds of information than other age groups. Knowing this from the collected data can help to streamline small and large marketing campaign making the promotional process more efficient.

Some decisions could have far more long-term effects. This is especially true with respect to the planning processes. Comprehensive planning does not occur in a vacuum. Planning, in its essence, is geared to develop programs, activities, and facilities that can serve a particular community. A community is also not the sum total of special interest groups that show up for public hearings. Planning, particularly for tax-based agencies, should take into account the various needs and interests of the various demographic sections that are served. The only scientific and defensible way to gather information of a large community of current users and potential future users, is to be able to estimate the needs of the entire community regardless of their level of usage of recreation or their decibel level in presenting a one-sided perspective in public meetings. Given that all comprehensive planning should attend to a wide range of needs, it is imperative that master planning be initiated with a rigorous process of data collection. Much of the planning decisions eventually rest on the specific kinds of information collected from the community. For instance, if the citizen data suggest that there is a greater need for neighborhood parks and facilities than for a single centralized facility in the community, then the planning decision must be geared toward providing for that need as opposed to needs expressed by members of special interest groups who rave and rant at public meetings.

The data collected from citizens helps to provide a sober and scientific response to the information collected in biased public meetings and workshops favored by planning consultants. It is important for the decision makers at recreation agencies to recognize that long-term planning decisions need to rely on the scientifically collected data from citizens as opposed to a few public meetings. In an age where accountability is critical, it is therefore imperative that agencies use the data when making decisions related to comprehensive planning. In the end, data collected from the citizens can help in better decisions related to the planning process. The addition of value to the decision-making process is specially important to note since the cost associated with the process of collecting data is often a small fraction of the budget for a parks and recreation agency, and the needs assessment is also often a small fraction of the comprehensive planning budget. But that little expense at the beginning of the data-collection process can help to save a lot of money in the actual planning and implementation phase. Indeed, the economic impact of collecting citizen data needs to be placed within the greater context of the costs involved with many planning decisions made by a recreation agency.

The data from citizens can provide a financial advantage in variety of ways. Knowing what the community wants can allow a department to rethink its programming and might even lead to the phasing out of programs that are unpopular and unnecessary based on the data. This can lead to some savings. It can also allow the department to understand where the needs are and based on the data from the community the department can begin to reconsider user fees that can be charged thus allowing the department to use the citizen data to understand where it can gain revenue. Moreover, departments that are in the process of applying for state and federal grants can strengthen their application by demonstrating that the department has collected objective data to support the need for funds. Simply put, it makes financial sense to spend a small amount of money to collect citizen-based information that will help to plan the spending of huge sums of money to build new resources, programs and facilities which are eventually meant to serve the citizens. There is indeed a democratic ethical call for going through a scientific process of asking taxpayers how they want their money spent. Consequently, an honest effort to collect citizen data also creates a positive image for a recreation agency since it demonstrates that the agency is willing and able to involve the community in the process of making decisions.

Public Face

The way in which a recreation agency approaches the process of collecting data from citizens also gives the agency an opportunity to create its own "face" in the community. The process of creating a presence, a face, and an image are interrelated activities where the agency must be able to present itself as a responsible and responsive public service. It is well known that recreation agencies have to compete with other public services like police and fire departments, and the better a recreation agency is able to present itself to its community the more likely it is that the agency will be able to garner the support of its constituency and maintain its financial status. This is being written at a time when America has witnessed one of the most difficult financial periods since the 1930s, and within the financial environment of the close of the first decade of the 21st century, it has become even more important for a recreation agency to create its face and maintain a positive image.

One of the ways in which this face is produced is through the process of collecting data from the citizens. The very fact that a government agency is responsive to the community offers an advantage to the agency. It is often the opinion of the public that government agencies operate on their own without ample attention to the needs of the people they serve. Education boards are plagued with complaints and city councils are often harangued for making decisions that the community feels are out of touch with the priorities of the community. This general distrust for government can be reversed when an agency makes a formal and earnest effort to collect information from the public. Recreation agencies can gain that advantage by starting the process of collecting input.

The specific method outlined here also offers many opportunities for creating the positive image. The focus group meetings, even when they are not moderated by the staff of the agency, offer an opportunity for the agency to interact with numerous different community groups. Many such groups might have never had direct contact with the recreation agency and its staff, but the arrangement of the focus group meetings offers that opportunity. These meetings play a very important role of creating a public outreach where there can be direct contact with members of the community. The actual data-collection process also places the agency before a large number of people in the community. The random sampling used in mail data collection usually includes people who could be unfamiliar with the agency. However, when such people receive the questionnaire, it develops a small degree of awareness about the agency. It is also often the case that agencies work with local media to promote the study. Media stories resulting from such efforts allow some positive exposure for the agency as long as the process of data collection is done correctly and does not attract criticism from the media. This is often avoided if a reputable scientist is involved in the process of data collection, which allows the agency to promote its data-collection efforts as legitimate and reliable as discussed earlier. In the case of web-based data collection, the agency has the opportunity to promote its website, which should have the "link" to the questionnaire. Those who complete the questionnaire would have to begin by visiting the website of the agency. It is also a good idea to direct the visitor back to the website of the agency after the respondent has completed the web-based questionnaire.

The opportunity of creating a public face and a positive image continues even after data collection has been completed when the agency can use the collected data and the analysis and report it via public meetings. The community can then get involved with interpreting the data and helping with the specific action plans that are generated by the data. These plans no longer appear as arbitrary plans developed by the agency staff or a planning consultant, but indeed are plans that are based on the needs expressed by the community that would benefit from the execution of the action plans.

Action Plans

I have pointed toward the relationship between collecting citizen input and planning throughout this book. It is important to keep sight of the fact that the process of collecting citizen input has an intrinsic value by offering an agency the chance to highlight and showcase its interest in community outreach. The data obtained from the process informs all levels of the planning process from short-term plans on how to handle specific issues related to individual programs and facilities. For instance, if it becomes evident that there are concerns related to perceptions of safety at a specific facility, then the agency could take some steps to rapidly address those issues and demonstrate responsive to the community. The data obviously plays a significant role in long-term planning for the agency because the responses help to lay out the road map for the agency for at least as long as there are no significant shifts in the demographic composition of a community. The data, however, needs to be interpreted appropriately and then the results need to be converted to action items that can be implemented using a staggered time line—some happening immediately and others happening slowly.

The conversion of the data to action items is a collaborative process where all the different players must contribute. The key researchers who collect and analyze the data are able to ensure that the data is correctly interpreted. They are the ones who must consider the different analytical options that can be used to answer specific questions. For instance, the researcher must be able to apply the correct statistical tool to the data to get the most information from the data. The agency practitioners are the ones who must be able to ask the pragmatic questions that the researcher can answer by analyzing the data. These questions need not be structured as abstract statistical questions, but should be questions that help to develop an action item. For instance, the marketing manager might want to streamline a specific campaign for maximum impact by reaching the audience who is most likely to participate in the activity. In such a situation, the researcher would look into the data and help the marketing manager to do the job best. The action items could also come from the public stakeholders who might have specific interests in the data to see how a volunteer effort might turn out. There the questions could come from the public and the action items could be developed by the public.

In the end, the process of collecting citizen data really is about making sure that the data is used for the benefit of the citizens who are served by a community recreation agency. There are some instances where the process of collecting citizen input takes on a more focused approach where the interest lies in specific kinds of populations. The next chapter considers some such conditions.

12

Special Applications

The discussion in this book has focused primarily on conducting citizen data from a community of people where the focus is on the entire population independent of any special characteristics of the people. There are situations where it becomes necessary to collect data from smaller groups of people who are defined by some special characteristics. Generally, the process of collecting data does not change significantly from what has been described thus far in the book, but it is useful to consider some of the adjustments that need to be done to meet the context of the research objective. The starting point of making the adjustments is to carefully examine the specific circumstance of the research and in this chapter some of the more common circumstances are examined.

Evaluation

One common condition of research is evaluating the efficacy of a specific recreation program. This kind of research is narrower in scope where the key research question deals with a specific and well-defined set of recreation programs and issues with the objective of measuring how the users of the programs responded to the program. At the simplest level, this can be considered to be a customer satisfaction study where the agency simply wants to know if the customers of a program or facility were satisfied with the program or facility. The questionnaire for such studies is a simple tool that only addresses the issues that are relevant to a specific program or facility. There is no need to ask questions that would not have any impact on the evaluation of the specific program. Usually such studies also require little specialized sample designs. Since the objective is to measure satisfaction with a specific program, it is often possible to find the contact information of all the people who might have participated in the program and then gather data from all the participants. Web-based data-collection technologies are well suited for these kinds of studies because it is possible to keep record of e-mail addresses of participants and invite them to complete a questionnaire on the Web.

Studies like this are also most effective when they are done on a longitudinal basis to measure how satisfaction of the customers might be changing with time. Such study designs could poll the same group of users who regularly use a facility and measure how their satisfaction might be changing as specific changes might be made to the facility. Programs can also be evaluated to see if there are differences based on the staff who offers the program. Collecting evaluation data over a long period of time allows a recreation agency to maintain a high quality of service that best serves the users.

One-time Decision Making

While evaluation studies benefit from longitudinality by tracking changes in behavior and attitudes over lengths of time to better serve the people who are users of the facility or program, there are situations where a recreation agency might have to make a one-time decision about a specific location or program. This happens most often with facilities that might have been freshly acquired by a recreation agency and it becomes important to decide how the facility would be used. In such cases, it is important to design a study that is focused on the specific facility and design a questionnaire that only deals with the specific facility. Usually, such questionnaires are shorter and require fewer focus group meetings since the scope of data collection is restricted to only the items that are important and relevant to the specific program or facility.

These studies require careful sample design that is similar to the larger scale citizen data collection studies. Unless there are convincing reasons to believe that the specific facility will only be used by a small and special group of people, the sample design must include all the citizens and the data collection process must be similar to the standard methods to collect data from an entire community. These studies are also not repeated often since the collected data helps to plan for the facility or program. Ongoing evaluation studies could help to measure the efficacy of the program or facility, but that would use the design described in the earlier section.

Many of the processes described in this book can also be applied to specific conditions of data collection where unique groups become the focus. The methodology in such cases remains independent of the type of people from whom data is collected and the protocol of data collection should remain valid and reliable.

Special Groups

One group that has become rightfully the center of attention is those who have special needs. People with disabilities who require inclusive recreation have come to the attention of recreation providers as agencies are recognizing the special needs recreation needs to be actively developed. This has led to an interest in collecting data specifically from people with special needs. Such data-collection efforts pose a few challenges. The first concern is with the design of the questionnaire. Traditional focus groups might not be sufficient for the questionnaire design process. Often members of the target population are unable to participate fully in focus group meetings. This requires the cooperation of proxies who can speak for and about the issues faced by the specific population. In such cases, the caregivers and family members could become the key spokespersons who participate in the focus group meetings and the researcher must spend some time understanding the issues of the population to be able to create a data-collection instrument that would serve the purpose of the study. The process of data collection might also have to be adjusted to ensure that members of the target population indeed are able to participate in the data-collection process. Traditional methods of self-response data collection using mailed questionnaires might have to be supplemented with other forms of data collection including face to face and telephone calls. Often the selected individual might not be able to participate in the data-collection process at all based on the level of functionality of the person, and in such cases, reliable proxies must be selected to provide the responses. It is possible to create relatively reliable samples for special needs populations because many national vendors of samples have such special samples now available for purchase. Sometimes the random sampling technique could be supplemented with network sampling methods where a person with special needs becomes the node for finding other people with disabilities who in turn become nodes to find yet more people with special needs. People with special needs often have shared support systems like Special Olympics, and thus it is often possible to locate the target population through network sampling strategies. Naturally, such techniques require a careful data-analysis process to account for the different probabilities of selection of the members of the population.

It could also be necessary to collect data from specific age groups. Much of the data-collection efforts described in this book deal with people who are over 18 years old. However, there is often a need to collect data from the younger population to compare the needs of the youth with those of adults. In such cases, it is important to conduct focus group meetings with the youth to ensure that their issues are included in the questionnaire. It is also important to ensure that the questionnaire is designed appropriately to account for the fact that younger people would be reading and responding to the questionnaire. Generally, the questionnaire for the youth is simpler and shorter than those used with adults. However, it is also important to ensure that the youth themselves respond to the questionnaire without interference from adult family members. Often this is best achieved by doing the data collection at a central location such as a middle or high school. That also results in the selection of a convenience sample because it could become very cumbersome to select a true random sample using specific locations. Typically, the questionnaires would be distributed to a selection of students in the school who would complete the questionnaire and return it to the researcher without taking the questionnaire home. In most youth studies, it is important to obtain the cooperation of the local school system so that data collection can be conducted in schools. It is inappropriate to do data collection in recreation centers or any facility or program operated by the recreation agency, because that process necessarily excludes those children who do not participate in agency activities. The school-based data-collection allows non-participants to be included in the data-collection process.

In the end, it is important to note that there are occasions where the standard methods of reliable data collection need to be modified to address the special conditions of data collection. In such cases it is important to maintain the overall integrity of the data-collection process to ensure that high-quality data is being produced by the process. It is incorrect to compromise the process just to be expedient and eventually end up with useless data.

At the same time, it might be impossible to maintain the complete protocol of reliable data collection. In such cases, it is important for the researcher to recognize the points at which specific compromises needed to be made. These result in specific limitations to the value of the data. For example, if in a youth data-collection process, none of the independent schools in a community were included in the sampling process, then that limitation must be clearly mentioned along with the findings from the limited study. Indeed, such limitations might exist in other studies, including those that masquerade as reliable data-collection efforts. It is an obligation of the researcher to point toward such limitations so that others who might be considering the data are aware that some aspects of the data might not be completely dependable. Sometimes these limitations are completely unavoidable and are fully accepted by those examining the data making it particularly important to clearly point towards limitations that happen most often in data-collection efforts that involve special conditions as described in this chapter.

Appendix A

Adult Questionnaire

RECREATION INTERESTS

Listed below are many different categories of recreational activities that can be enjoyed year-round. For each activity, please circle whether YOU and/or your family would have **interest** *in the activities.*

Category	Example	Great Interest	Some Interest	No Interest
Aquatics	Lap swim, swim lessons, open swim, water park, swim team, etc.	3	2	1
Arts & Crafts	Ceramics, photography, drawing, painting, textiles, etc.	3	2	1
Environmental	Gardening, natural landscaping, nature walks, etc.	3	2	1
Family Programs	Splash parties and parent/child dances	3	2	1
Hobbies	Cooking, flower arranging, models, chess, etc.	3	2	1
Golf	Junior golf, driving range, etc.	3	2	1
Indoor Fitness	Exercise equipment, free weights, jogging track, etc.	3	2	1
Outdoor Fitness	Hiking, running, walking, biking, etc.	3	2	1
Performing Arts	Theater, concerts, ballet, music, dance, etc.	3	2	1
Self-Improvement	Self-defense, home, home computer, etc.	3	2	1
Social	Dancing, teen clubs, senior club, bridge, etc.	3	2	1
Special Events	One or two day events, festivals, shows, etc.	3	2	1
Special Needs Programs	Special Olympics, therapeutic recreation, etc.	3	2	1
Sports & Athletics	Baseball, soccer, basketball, football etc.	3	2	1
Travel & Tourism	Trips to points of interest within 3 hour drive, etc.	3	2	1

AREAS OF EMPHASIS

Please circle whether the following additional facilities and programs are needed for the children, teens, adults and seniors in your family.

	Yes	No		Yes	No
Activities for youth	1	2	Junior golf	1	2
Activity rooms (such as for crafts)	1	2	Kickball	1	2
Athletic fields	1	2	Kiddie pool	1	2
After-school and summer program space	1	2	Larger facility	1	2
Aquatic facility	1	2	Larger gymnasium	1	2
Area for summer program	1	2	Larger multi-use rooms	1	2
Artificial turf fields	1	2	Shaded areas in pools and fields	1	2
Badminton	1	2	Movie night	1	2
Basketball practice court	1	2	Outdoor basketball courts	1	2
Bigger pool facility	1	2	Park lighting	1	2
Bigger weight room	1	2	Picnic areas	1	2
Biking trail	1	2	Restroom facilities at parks	1	2
Bowling alley	1	2	Security at facility	1	2
Cheerleading	1	2	Skate park	1	2
Computer room	1	2	Spectator seating	1	2
Concession stands	1	2	Tennis courts	1	2
Dance lessons	1	2	Theater space	1	2
Dance/jazzexercise room	1	2	Trainers for exercise	1	2
Family pool	1	2	Traveling athletic teams	1	2
Cooling in the gymnasium	1	2	Video surveillance camera	1	2
Football fields	1	2	Volleyball courts indoor/outdoor	1	2
Game room	1	2	Volunteerism	1	2
Gymnastics	1	2	Water exercise	1	2
Indoor racquetball courts	1	2	Zero depth pool	1	2
Other:	1	2	Other:	1	2

TIME AND ATTENDANCE

The Miami Springs Parks and Recreation Department wants to schedule recreational activities and special events when it is most convenient for you and your family. Please circle all the times when you and your family would attend recreation activities, programs and facilities.

	ADULTS							YOUTH						
	M	T	W	Th	F	Sa	S	M	T	W	Th	F	Sa	S
6 a.m. - 8 a.m.	1	2	3	4	5	6	7	1	2	3	4	5	6	7
8 a.m. - Noon	1	2	3	4	5	6	7	1	2	3	4	5	6	7
Noon – 4 p.m.	1	2	3	4	5	6	7	1	2	3	4	5	6	7
4 p.m. - 7 p.m.	1	2	3	4	5	6	7	1	2	3	4	5	6	7
7 p.m. - 11 p.m.	1	2	3	4	5	6	7	1	2	3	4	5	6	7
11 p.m. - 6 a.m.	1	2	3	4	5	6	7	1	2	3	4	5	6	7

Please indicate by writing in a number approximately how many times YOU and/or your family visited/attended the following facilities in the past 12 months.

	0	1-2	3-5	6-8	9-12	More than 12
Bike Paths						
Dog Park						
Golf Course						
Gymnasium						
Pool						
Prince Field's Tot Lot						
Tennis/Racquetball Courts						
Theater						
Fitness/Weight Room						
Other parks						

*There are some reasons why people cannot, or do not, participate in programs, or visit sites offered by the Miami Springs Parks and Recreation Department. Please circle the reasons why YOU and/or your family have **not** participated.*

	Yes		Yes
Cost	1	Not accessible for the disabled	1
Inconvenient timing	1	Not interested in public recreation	1
Lack of cleanliness	1	Parking not adequate	1
Lack of information	1	Poor customer service	1
Lack of maintenance	1	Poor quality of program	1
Lack of qualified staffing	1	Safety concerns	1
Lack of restrooms	1	Substandard old facilities	1
Facilities are too small	1	The facilities are too crowded	1
Old condition of the building	1	Other:	1

PERSONAL OPINIONS

The Miami Springs Parks and Recreation Department would like to obtain your personal opinions about a variety of issues. Please circle the number that most closely reflects your attitudes.

	Strongly Agree	Agree	Disagree	Strongly Disagree	Don't Know
In general, the facilities that I have visited satisfy my needs	4	3	2	1	8
The Miami Springs Parks and Recreation Department is responsive to community recreation needs	4	3	2	1	8
The park facilities I visit are clean and well maintained	4	3	2	1	8
The quality of leadership/supervision provided by the Miami Springs Parks and Recreation Department is good	4	3	2	1	8
The Miami Springs Parks and Recreation Department staff is courteous and helpful	4	3	2	1	8
I am aware of the recreation programs and activities the Miami Springs Parks and Recreation Department offers	4	3	2	1	8
I feel safe in the parks	4	3	2	1	8
There is a need for more activities for people with disabilities	4	3	2	1	8
I prefer neighborhood parks over a large centralized park	4	3	2	1	8
The Miami Springs Parks and Recreation Department recreation activities are primarily tailored for the youth	4	3	2	1	8
The Miami Springs Parks and Recreation Department recreation activities are primarily tailored for adults	4	3	2	1	8
There is a need for special programs for persons over age 55	4	3	2	1	8
The existence of well-maintained parks adds to the quality of life in the community	4	3	2	1	8
The Miami Springs Parks and Recreation Department should provide more activities where the whole family can participate	4	3	2	1	8
I am satisfied with the recreation opportunities I receive for my tax dollars	4	3	2	1	8
I am willing to pay reasonable users fees for new recreation opportunities	4	3	2	1	8
The parks I visit are conveniently located	4	3	2	1	8
The Miami Springs Parks and Recreation Department office hours are convenient	4	3	2	1	8
The children's park and senior center should not be next to each other	4	3	2	1	8
It is better to have a centralized multi-use facility rather than many small facilities	4	3	2	1	8

INFORMATION ABOUT PARKS AND RECREATION OPPORTUNITIES

We are interested in determining the best ways of informing you about parks and recreation programs and activities. Please circle the appropriate numbers below to indicate how effective the method is.

	Very Effective	Effective	Not Sure	Ineffective	Very Ineffective
Brochures, flyers or posters at public facilities	5	4	3	2	1
Cable TV (Channel 77)	5	4	3	2	1
Direct mail of program book	5	4	3	2	1
E-mailed announcement	5	4	3	2	1
Website	5	4	3	2	1
Newspaper	5	4	3	2	1
Flyers at local businesses	5	4	3	2	1
Word of mouth	5	4	3	2	1
Handouts through schools	5	4	3	2	1

GENERAL INFORMATION

Please help us make better decisions by providing the following information. Please remember that the individual answers will be treated with confidence. Please circle the number of the response or fill in the blank.

What is your gender?   **What is your age?**
Male....1   Female....2   18-24...1   25-34...2   35-44...3   45-54...4
                                         55-64...5   65-69...6   70-74...7   Over 75...8

What was your household income before taxes in 2006?
Under $24,999.........1 $25,000 to $49,999.....2 $50,000 to $74,999....3 $75,000 to $99,999.......4
$100,000 to $124,900 ...5   Over $125,000 6

How many adults, including yourself, age 19 and above, currently live in your household? ____

How many children in your household are: under age five ____; ages 5 to 10 ____; ages 11 to 14 ____; ages 15 to 18 ____

What is your marital status:
Married...1   Divorced/Separated...2   Single...3

What is your current employment status:
Full time...1   Part time...2   Not employed...3

What kind of school do the children in your home go to (indicate only one answer):
Public School...1   Private School...2   Home School...3   No school age child...4

What is the highest level of education obtained by you?
No school completed...1   Elementary school...2   Middle school...3   High school...4
Some college (no degree)...5   Associate degree...6   Bachelors degree...7   Graduate or post-graduate degree...8

How many years have you lived in Miami Springs? ____

How long would you plan to stay in Miami Springs? ____

What is your ethnicity?
Caucasian...1   African-American...2   Hispanic...3   Asian...4
Other (Specify) _____

Do you use the Internet at: Home...1   Work...2   Home and Work...3   No access...4

Do you, or anyone in your household have any disabilities? Yes...1 No...2

Looking at the map on the back of the cover letter, please put in the number for your area of residence: _____

THANK YOU FOR YOUR COOPERATION AND PLEASE WRITE DOWN ANY ADDITIONAL COMMENTS YOU MAY HAVE IN THE SPACE BELOW

Appendix B

Youth Questionnaire

RECREATION INTERESTS

*Listed below are many different categories of recreational activities that can be enjoyed year-round. For each activity, please circle whether YOU and/or your family would have **interest** in the activities.*

Category	Example	Great Interest	Some Interest	No Interest
Aquatics	Lap swim, swim lessons, open swim, water park, swim team, etc.	3	2	1
Arts & Crafts	Ceramics, photography, drawing, painting, textiles, etc.	3	2	1
Environmental	Gardening, natural landscaping, nature walks, etc.	3	2	1
Family Programs	Splash parties and parent/child dances	3	2	1
Hobbies	Cooking, flower arranging, models, chess, etc.	3	2	1
Golf	Junior golf, driving range, etc.	3	2	1
Indoor Fitness	Exercise equipment, free weights, jogging track, etc.	3	2	1
Outdoor Fitness	Hiking, running, walking, biking, etc.	3	2	1
Performing Arts	Theater, concerts, ballet, music, dance, etc.	3	2	1
Self-Improvement	Self-defense, home, home computer, etc.	3	2	1
Social	Dancing, teen clubs, senior club, bridge, etc.	3	2	1
Special Events	One or two day events, festivals, shows, etc.	3	2	1
Special Needs Programs	Special Olympics, therapeutic recreation, etc.	3	2	1
Sports & Athletics	Baseball, soccer, basketball, football etc.	3	2	1
Travel & Tourism	Trips to points of interest within 3 hour drive, etc.	3	2	1

AREAS OF EMPHASIS

Please circle whether the following additional facilities and programs are needed for the children, teens, adults and seniors in your family.

	Yes	No		Yes	No
Activities for youth	1	2	Junior golf	1	2
Activity rooms (such as for crafts)	1	2	Kickball	1	2
Athletic fields	1	2	Kiddie pool	1	2
After-school and summer program space	1	2	Larger facility	1	2
Aquatic facility	1	2	Larger gymnasium	1	2
Area for summer program	1	2	Larger multi-use rooms	1	2
Artificial turf fields	1	2	Shaded areas in pools and fields	1	2
Badminton	1	2	Movie night	1	2
Basketball practice court	1	2	Outdoor basketball courts	1	2
Bigger pool facility	1	2	Park lighting	1	2
Bigger weight room	1	2	Picnic areas	1	2
Biking trail	1	2	Restroom facilities at parks	1	2
Bowling alley	1	2	Security at facility	1	2
Cheerleading	1	2	Skate park	1	2
Computer room	1	2	Spectator seating	1	2
Concession stands	1	2	Tennis courts	1	2
Dance lessons	1	2	Theater space	1	2
Dance/jazzexercise room	1	2	Trainers for exercise	1	2
Family pool	1	2	Traveling athletic teams	1	2
Cooling in the gymnasium	1	2	Video surveillance camera	1	2
Football fields	1	2	Volleyball courts indoor/outdoor	1	2
Game room	1	2	Volunteerism	1	2
Gymnastics	1	2	Water exercise	1	2
Indoor racquetball courts	1	2	Zero depth pool	1	2
Other:	1	2	Other:	1	2

TIME AND ATTENDANCE

Please indicate by writing in a number approximately how many times YOU and/or your family visited/attended the following facilities in the past 12 months.

	0	1-2	3-5	6-8	9-12	More than 12
Bike Paths						
Gymnasium						
Pool						
Tennis/Racquetball Courts						
Theater						
Fitness/Weight Room						
Other parks						

*There are some reasons why people cannot, or do not, participate in programs, or visit sites offered by the Miami Springs Parks and Recreation Department. Please circle the reasons why YOU and/or your family have **not** participated.*

	Yes		Yes
Cost	1	Facilities are too small	1
Inconvenient timing	1	Old condition of the building	1
Lack of cleanliness	1	Poor customer service	1
Lack of information	1	Poor quality of program	1
Lack of maintenance	1	Safety concerns	1
Lack of qualified staffing	1	Substandard old facilities	1
Lack of restrooms	1	The facilities are too crowded	1

PERSONAL OPINIONS

The Miami Springs Parks and Recreation Department would like to obtain your personal opinions about a variety of issues. Please circle the number that most closely reflects your attitudes.

	Strongly Agree	Agree	Disagree	Strongly Disagree	Don't Know
In general, the facilities that I have visited satisfy my needs	4	3	2	1	8
The park facilities I visit are clean and well maintained	4	3	2	1	8
The Miami Springs Parks and Recreation Department staff is courteous and helpful	4	3	2	1	8
I am aware of the recreation programs and activities the Miami Springs Parks and Recreation Department offers	4	3	2	1	8
I feel safe in the parks	4	3	2	1	8
The existence of well-maintained parks adds to the quality of life in the community	4	3	2	1	8
The Miami Springs Parks and Recreation Department should provide more activities where the whole family can participate	4	3	2	1	8
The children's park and senior center should not be next to each other	4	3	2	1	8
It is better to have a centralized multi-use facility rather than many small facilities	4	3	2	1	8

GENERAL INFORMATION

To help us make better decisions, please tell us a little bit about you.

What is your gender?   **What is your grade in school?**

Male....1   Female....2   Grade 7   Grade 8   Grade 9   Grade 10

Grade 11   Grade 12

THANK YOU FOR COMPLETING THE QUESTIONNAIRE!

Appendix C

Questionnaire Cover Letter

Dear Sir or Madam:

In continuing our commitment to provide quality leisure and recreational services, the Battle Creek Parks and Recreation Department has contracted Management Learning Laboratories of Winston-Salem, NC, to conduct a community needs assessment to judge the recreation and leisure needs of Battle Creek residents. This survey will be used as one of several tools in the development of the City's plans for providing recreation and leisure services in Battle Creek.

It is with much enthusiasm that the City submits this survey to you and other Battle Creek residents who have been scientifically selected by a random sampling technique to represent the community.

Please take a few moments from your busy schedule to read the instructions of each section carefully and respond accordingly. We ask that only an adult residing in the household complete the survey. It is important that you return the questionnaire to MLL in the envelope provided. Please return the survey within two weeks. Names are not requested, and individual responses are strictly confidential. If you need assistance with completing the questionnaire please feel free to call MLL at 877-789-5247.

We extend our sincere appreciation for your participation in this survey and thank you for your continued support in the growth and development of Battle Creek.

Appendix D

Survey Map

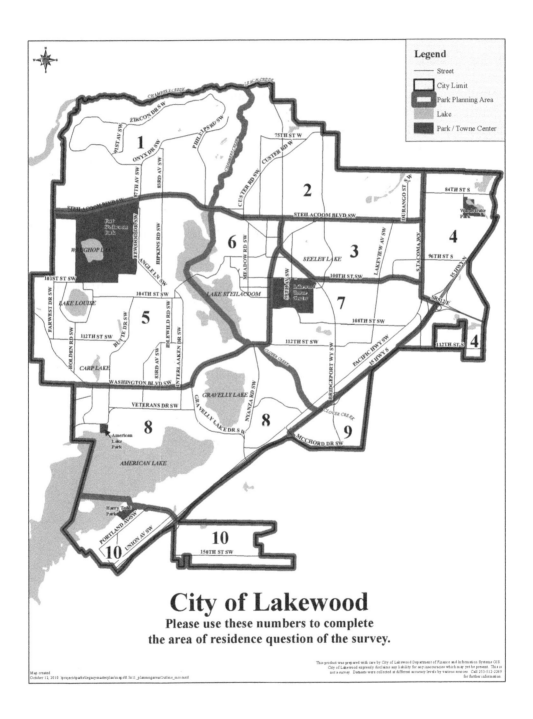

City of Lakewood
Please use these numbers to complete
the area of residence question of the survey.

Appendix E

Outgoing envelope

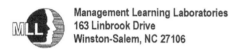

Management Learning Laboratories
163 Linbrook Drive
Winston-Salem, NC 27106

Help Norman plan for the
future of Ruby Grant Park

Appendix F

Reminder Postcard

Dear Friend:

Have you voiced your opinion yet about the future of parks and recreation programs in Lakewood?

About a week ago, you received a questionnaire on behalf of the Parks, Recreation and Community Services Department.   If you've already completed and returned this questionnaire, thank you. If not, please take a few minutes to give us your opinions and return the survey in the envelope provided.

Thank you for your time!   Your feedback will give us guidance in developing parks and recreation programs that will benefit Lakewood for years to come.

Sincerely,

City Manager

Appendix G

Web-based Questionnaire

Default Section

Please indicate how many times in the past 12 months you and/or another member of your family utilized the following facilities and/or programs.

	Never	Once	1 to 6 times	7 to 12 times	13 to 24 times	26 times or more
Arts and Crafts (e.g., oil painting class)						
Coolwell Community Center						
County Parks						
Health and wellness (e.g., aerobics)						
Lakes						
Outdoor programming (e.g., nature hikes)						
Senior Programming (e.g., senior bingo)						
Special Events (e.g., fall festival)						
Trails						
Youth Sports (e.g., youth basketball)						

Other (please specify)

(Next)

Please indicate if the following are barriers to participation in Amherst County Recreation and Parks Department (ACRPD) programs & facilities

	Yes	No
Better facilities are available elsewhere	☐	☐
Cost	☐	☐
Difficulties with registration	☐	☐
Inconvenient location	☐	☐
Inconvenient timing of activities	☐	☐
Lack of cleanliness	☐	☐
Lack of information	☐	☐
Lack of maintenance	☐	☐
Lack of restrooms	☐	☐
Nothing of interest is offered	☐	☐
Transportation	☐	☐

Other (please specify)

```
[                                              ]
```

(Prev)(Next)

Please indicate how effective the following methods would be for keeping you informed.

	Effective	Not Sure	Ineffective
Cell phone/phone messages	◡	◡	◡
Department Website	◡	◡	◡
E-mail announcements	◡	◡	◡
Flyers in public places	◡	◡	◡
Flyers in schools	◡	◡	◡
MySpace/Facebook, etc.	◡	◡	◡
Newspaper ads	◡	◡	◡
Radio ads	◡	◡	◡
Word of mouth	◡	◡	◡

Other (please specify)

(Prev) (Next)

The ACRPD wants to schedule recreation activities and special events when it is most convenient for you and your family. Please circle all the times when the adults in your family are available to attend recreation activities, programs and facilities.

	Monday	Tueasday	Wednesday	Thursday	Friday	Saturday	Sunday
6 a.m. - 8 a.m.							
8 a.m. - Noon							
Noon – 4 p.m.							
4 p.m. - 7 p.m.							
7 p.m. - 11 p.m.							
11 p.m. - 6 a.m.							

The ACRPD wants to schedule recreation activities and special events when it is most convenient for you and your family. Please circle all the times when the youth in your family are available to attend recreation activities, programs and facilities.

	Monday	Tueasday	Wednesday	Thursday	Friday	Saturday	Sunday
6 a.m. - 8 a.m.							
8 a.m. - Noon							
Noon – 4 p.m.							
4 p.m. - 7 p.m.							
7 p.m. - 11 p.m.							
11 p.m. - 6 a.m.							

Prev Next

Please indicate how important you feel the following facilities and programs are for the children, teens, adults and seniors in your family.

	Not Important	Important
A center for special events	⬤	⬤
After school programs	⬤	⬤
Amphitheater	⬤	⬤
Art in parks	⬤	⬤
Arts and crafts programs	⬤	⬤
Badminton	⬤	⬤
Baseball Fields	⬤	⬤
Basketball Courts	⬤	⬤
Bike Trails	⬤	⬤
Boating	⬤	⬤
Bowling Alley	⬤	⬤
Community gardens	⬤	⬤
Concerts in parks	⬤	⬤
Dance programs	⬤	⬤
Disc Golf	⬤	⬤
Educational programs and classes	⬤	⬤
Fitness center	⬤	⬤
Fitness Walking	⬤	⬤
Geo Caching	⬤	⬤
Horseshoes	⬤	⬤
More water-based activities	⬤	⬤
Neighborhood Parks	⬤	⬤
Outdoor movies	⬤	⬤
Picnicking	⬤	⬤
Picnic Shelters	⬤	⬤

The ACRPD would like to obtain your personal opinions about a variety of issues. Please indicate your opinions about the following.

	Strongly Agree	Agree	Disagree	Strongly Disagree	Don't Know
I am aware of the recreation programs and activities that are offered					
The Department staff are generally courteous and helpful					
I am satisfied with the recreation opportunities I receive for my tax dollars					
I am willing to pay reasonable user fees for recreation opportunities					
I prefer smaller parks closer to my home over a large centralized park					
I would volunteer for activities, programs, and projects					
It is easy to register for programs and activities					
The condition of athletic fields is satisfactory					
The quality of leadership/supervision provided is good					
There is a need for more recreation opportunities for people with disabilities					
There is a need for more teen programs					
There is a need for programs for persons over age 55					
Well-maintained parks add to the quality of life in the community					
The Department does a good job of maintaining parks in the community					
I prefer larger centralized parks to smaller parks closer to my home					
The programs and facilities are safe					

Other (please specify)

```


```

(Prev)(Next)

Gender

[⬍]

Age

[⬍]

Household Income

[⬍]

What is the highest level of education obtained by you?

[⬍]

What is your marital status?

[⬍]

What is your ethnicity?

[⬍]

Other (please specify)

[   ]

(Prev)(Done)

Appendix H

Reminder E-mail

Dear IES Abroad Student,

Congratulations on completing your IES Abroad study abroad program! We sincerely hope that it was a meaningful and fulfilling academic, cultural, and personal experience.

In an effort to continually improve our programs, we invite you to share your perceptions, comments, and suggestions about each element of the IES Abroad Direct Enrollment program. Your feedback is extremely valuable. We will use your responses to influence program development and to educate prospective students about IES Abroad Direct Enrollment programs.

Click on the link below to begin filling out the survey about your IES Abroad experience:

http://www.surveymonkey.com/s.aspx

This survey is used for evaluation and development purposes only. It will not affect your grades. Your responses are confidential. Please click on the link below if you do not wish to receive any more survey requests:

http://www.surveymonkey.com/optout.aspx

We hope you enjoyed your experience abroad, and we wish you the best of luck in the future!

The IES Team
https://www.iesabroad.org/IES/home.html

Appendix I

CompuRec

CompuRec is a program developed by Management Learning Laboratories that facilitates basic and complex statistical analysis of social science and public opinion data to generate frequency distributions, cross-tabulations, and other more sophisticated statistical analysis for understanding public opinion and attitudes. CompuRec is specifically aimed at busy recreation professionals who want quick access to baseline information about the communities that they serve. For instance, using the program the decision makers can instantaneously answer questions such as: "According to the study, what part of the community is least informed about recreation?" or "According to the study, what age group in the community has the greatest need for a community center?"

By using CompuRec, a practitioner does not need to code data or learn specific computer languages. CompuRec and the data collected in the survey are loaded into the agency computer by MLL, and the user is trained to use the program. However, since CompuRec is an expandable package, any user, after some experience, will be able to do sophisticated data analysis by going beyond the simple operations. With CompuRec, it would be possible for the City to "add on" any new data that may be collected in the future. It is a flexible and expandable system that offers the possibility of both complex analyses of the data to target specific user groups as well as new data collected from various user groups. The CompuRec data can also be integrated with existing GIS data since there is demographic information related to location that is collected in the questionnaire.

The following pages show examples of data that CompuRec can provide.

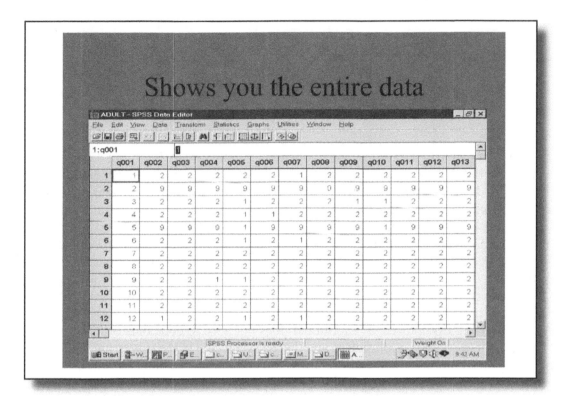

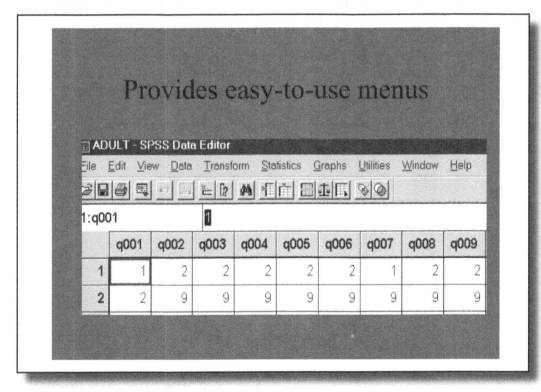

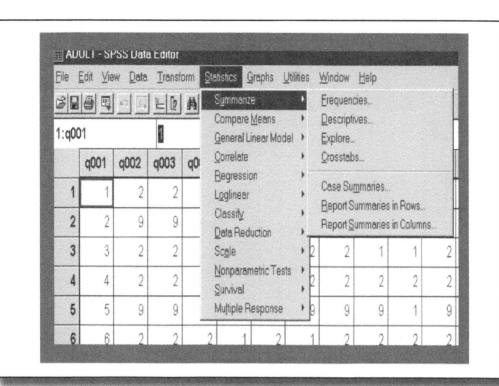

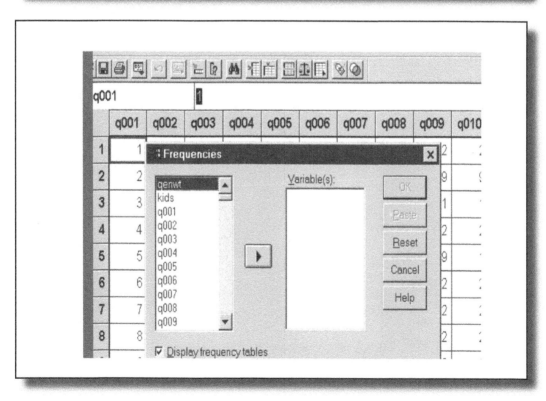

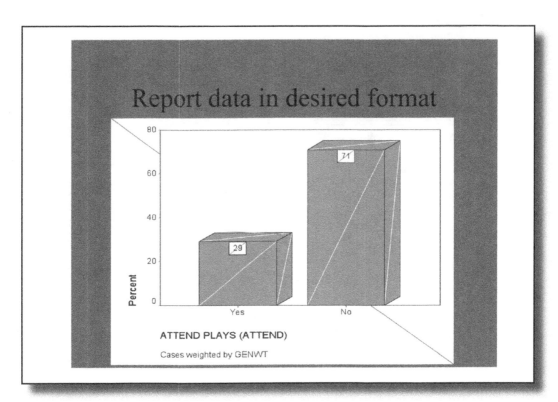

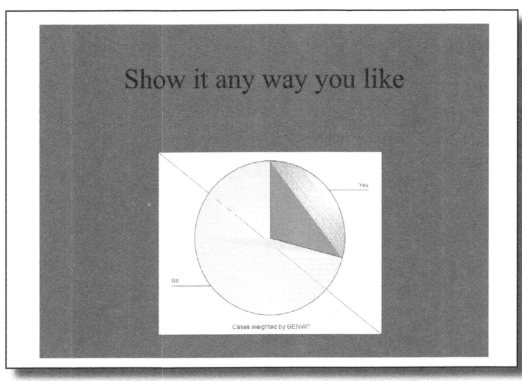

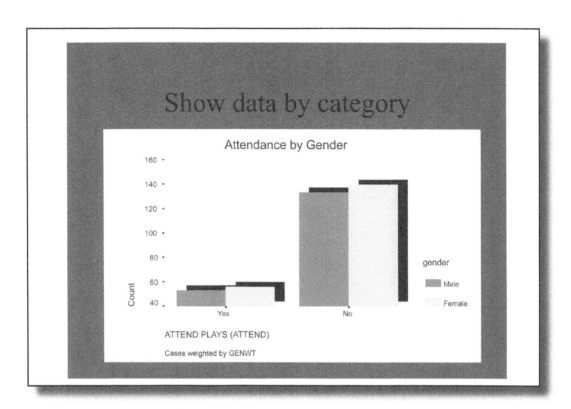

Resulting Recommendation

- Neither men nor women attend plays in this community. Perhaps more opportunities are required or there might not be enough interest in this activity.
- You can test that too!
- Let's create a graph of interest broken down by gender

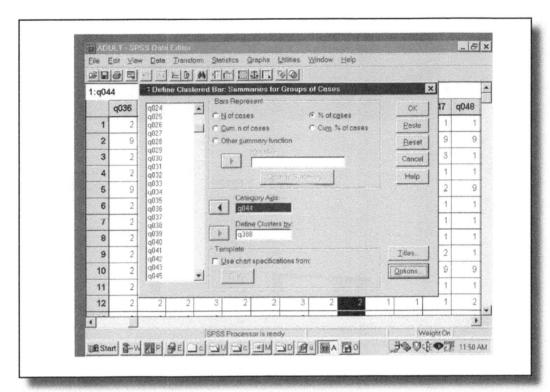

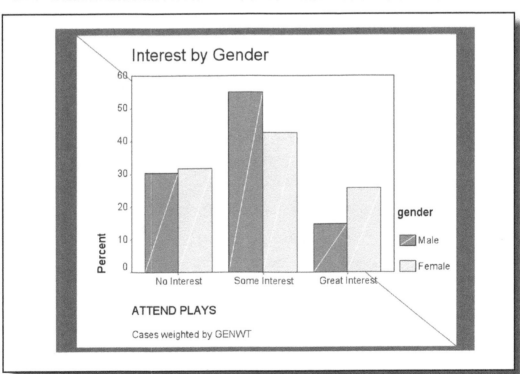

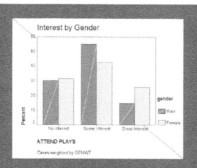

Now we see that women are more interested
than men

Conclusion:
**Women will attend more if they are given the
opportunity**

Produces instantaneous access to
data

ATTEND PLAYS (ATTEND)

		Frequency	Percent	Valid Percent	Cumulative Percent
Valid	Yes	115	25.4	29.1	29.1
	No	280	61.9	70.9	100.0
	Total	395	87.3	100.0	
Missing	9	58	12.7		
	Total	58	12.7		
Total		452	100.0		

Appendix J

Executive Summary

Method used in the needs assessment:
- Several focus group meetings with Lakewood officials, adult and youth citizens to formulate questionnaire.
- Interviews with City officials
- Mailing of questionnaires by direct U.S. mail resulting in a response rate of 12.1% with 490 usable questionnaires.
- Aggregate analysis of the data set

Major findings from adult random sample study
1. Nearly 82% of the respondents are interested in passive recreation such as sitting in the parks, enjoying scenery, etc.
2. More than 75% of the respondents are interested in fitness-related activities.
3. More than 89% of the respondents indicated a need for different kinds of trails.
4. Nearly 84% of the respondents were interested in indoor swimming opportunities.
5. Nearly 85% of the respondents expressed the importance of land acquisition.
6. Nearly all the respondents suggested that the top spending priorities should be maintenance of existing facilities, development of new parks and open space, and recreation centers.
7. Nearly all the respondents agreed that they would be more likely to visit the parks and facilities if they are clean and well maintained.
8. Nearly all of the respondents indicated that the department needs to provide activities for seniors.
9. Nearly 82% of the respondents agreed that they were willing to pay user fees.
10. Nearly half of the respondents indicated that weekday evenings were the best time for recreation activities.

Appendix K

Action Plan

This section of the report takes some of the key recommendations from each section of the report and suggests a plan of action for the MPT. Some of these can be achieved in the short term, while others need to be considered as long-term plan elements.

Maintenance of facilities: The results clearly suggest that the MPT needs to emphasize maintenance of its facilities and continue to provide high quality programming. The following recommendations address this issue:

- MPT should consider safety, cleanliness, and maintenance its highest priorities in order to ensure a positive perception of MPT facilities.
- MPT should ensure adequate restrooms and parking at its facilities, as well as lighting where possible.
- MPT should emphasize improvement of existing facilities over new ones and local neighborhood parks over a large centralized park.
- MPT should consider park and facility maintenance its highest priorities when budget decisions are made, while keeping in mind the importance of protecting and caring for open spaces.
- MPT should take location and willingness to travel into account when planning new parks or facilities or renovating existing ones.
- MPT should ensure that neighborhood park maintenance remains a high priority given the use of and appreciation for the parks in Tacoma.

Programming for families: The results clearly suggest that the "family" is important to the respondents and thus the MPT should consider the following recommendations as important components of its future plans:

- MPT should ensure it is offering some opportunities for parents and children to recreate together.
- MPT should provide family-oriented activities.
- MPT should provide opportunities for residents to enjoy movies and concerts in parks for reasonable fees, as well as other special.
- MPT should consider additional ways of accommodating the travel and tourism interests of the residents of Tacoma for reasonable user fees.

Emphasize the outdoor: MPT needs to place significant emphasis on environmental activities and outdoor activities. The results all support the following recommendations:

- MPT should ensure it provides opportunities and spaces for the residents to participate in activities related to the environment and outdoors.
- MPT should be aware of the environmental concerns of residents and take steps to protect open areas, as well as consider it acceptable to delay or reduce watering for environmental reasons.
- MPT should focus on facilities (supported by user fees) that enable residents to enjoy the outdoors, such as those that feature living and historical attractions, as well as outdoor pools.

Emphasize the person-fitness, self-improvement: The respondents suggest that there is a significant interest in self-improvement and fitness, the MPT needs to address those issues using the following recommendations:

- MPT should consider how it best can meet the athletic and aquatic needs of the residents of Tacoma.
- MPT should focus on ample athletic facilities for the residents of Tacoma.

Financial issues: The respondents had specific feelings about the way in which MPT should be funded and how its funding should be used. To that end, the MPT should consider adopting the following recommendations:

- MPT should ensure its fees are reasonable.
- MPT first should consider how it may find and take advantage of grants in providing relevant recreation opportunities to the residents of Tacoma.
- MPT should seek out corporate sponsorship and corporate and private donations, and to a lesser extent commercial activities, when possible.
- MPT should proceed with caution when considering taxes and bonds; these means of funding should be avoided unless MPT can significantly increase public support for them as being necessary in order to provide much-needed facilities and/or programming.
- MPT should consider taking advantage of user fees to provide arts and crafts programming, as well as other lessons and classes, where possible.
- MPT should consider park and facility maintenance its highest priorities when budget decisions are made, while keeping in mind the importance of protecting and caring for open spaces.

Administrative issues: Based on the data, the MPT should consider the following as recommendations for action with the respect to the way in which it performs its activities:

- MPT should ensure continued quality customer service as well as consider ways of keeping the residents of Tacoma well informed about recreation opportunities.
- MPT should consider the best ways of keeping residents informed, including e-mail for those residents who would like to take advantage of that medium.
- MPT should address perceptions of inequity and unresponsiveness where possible.
- MPT should do what it can to maintain and improve positive public perception of its staff.

Appendix L
Presentation Slides

The slides in this appendix summarize many of the ideas presented in this book, and these slides have been used at various regional recreation conferences as well at the annual conferences of the National Recreation and Park Association (NRPA).

Collecting Citizen Input

Ananda Mitra
NRPA 2010

Need for Data

- Cost savings by prioritizing
- Constantly changing needs
- New Capital opportunities
- Balancing resources
- Competition
- Maximizing Effect in Community
- External pressures

A nee
scier
statistica
unders
communit
needs, att
and beh
constituenc
recreation se

A Ne

...er.

•A needs assessment must not be confused with a master plan.

•A master plan can be developed after a needs assessment has been conducted.

•A needs assessment must be considered to be independent of a master plan.

Throughout this presentation it will be stressed that a needs assessment must be considered to be an independent study from a master plan, although the needs assessment can certainly be used as a blueprint for developing a master plan.

...ds Assessment is

- **NOT** Public meetings
- **NOT** Mailer going out with utility bills
- **NOT** Asking people questions at the swimming pool
- **NOT** Getting input from friends and family
- **NOT** Something that has not been done systematically

If any of the following are true:

- Plan to do a master plan in the next couple of years
- Plan to apply for state/federal funds
- You want to know what the community wants
- Planning staff need more community information

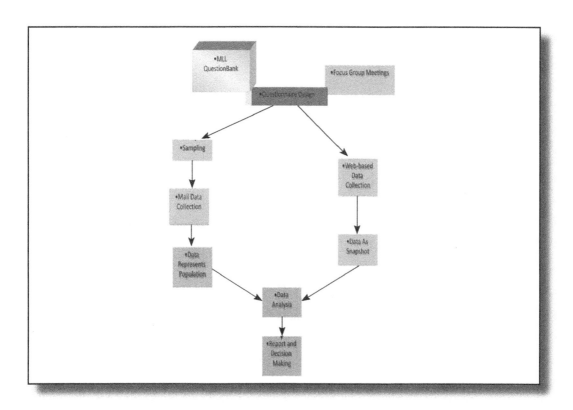

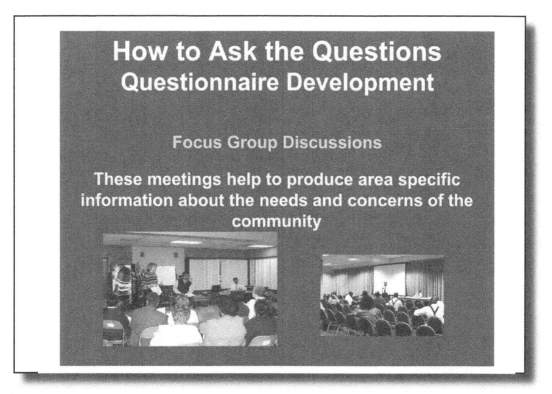

How to Ask the Questions
Questionnaire Development

Questionnaire Formatting

Considerable effort is spent in producing an instrument that is not only pleasing to the eye but easy to fill out as well

Cover Letter

The letter accompanying the questionnaire is carefully written to have the maximum impact

How to Ask the Questions
Sampling

Population Definition

The community to be surveyed is carefully defined in terms of residency requirements location, and other specific criteria

Sample Selection

A random sample is selected from the defined population. Random means that every member in the population has a chance of being selected

How to Ask the Questions
Data Collection

Mail Data Collection

The questionnaires are sent out by mail and
the respondents send them back by mail as well.
Self-addressed envelopes are provided

Response Rate (RR)

A minimum response rate of 20% to 25% is expected
on the first mailing. When necessary a second
mailing can be conducted to boost the RR

How to Ask the Questions
Data Collection

New Technologies

Web-based data collection offers:

On-going data collection
On-demand reports
Internal benchmarking
Inexpensive mode
Possibility of making policy decisions in time

Not a random sample
Internet access

Kiosks

Assumptions

- New tools offer different data-collection methods
- All the assumptions of good needs assessment research design remain the same
- The analysis of the data is no different from data collected using other methods
- Skill sets are nearly the same for other methods of data collection

Web-based data collection

- Convert the paper and pencil to html
- Find appropriate Web-space to host the survey
- Promote the survey to possible respondents
- Periodic data harvesting
- Interim reports
- Final report with longitudinal analysis

Data Analysis
CompuRec

As the master planning proceeds, the data can be constantly mined and analyzed

The system provides easy access to the data and helps to answer key questions about the data

Longitudinal Analysis

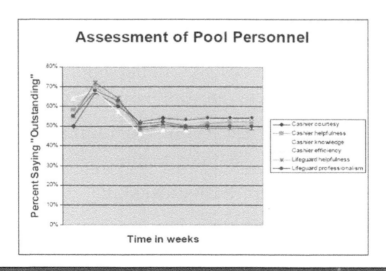

Skill Sets

- Communication – focus group facilitation
- Questionnaire design – understanding of the issues related to questionnaire design
- Management and Organization – coordination of the data-management process
- Data Analysis – Statistical skill
- Data Presentation

Skill Sets for Web-based data collection

- Communication – focus group facilitation
- Questionnaire design – understanding of the issues related to questionnaire design
- Internet expertise – html programming, survey hosting, data harvesting
- Data Analysis – Statistical skill
- Data Presentation

Costs

- Time – between 6 to 8 weeks
- Resources – staff and facilities
- Dollar – cost of printing, mailing, etc.
- Political – legitimacy, credibility

Outsourcing

- Timing – when to do the study
- One-stop shopping – pros and cons
- Regionality – local and national
- Process – from RFP to recommendations and data

Things to DO!

- Collect information from a large cross-section of the community.
- Collect information about all the different aspects of leisure - attitudes, use, behavior
- Always ask the demographic questions
- Remember "user" data is different from "community" data

Things NOT to DO!

- Depend only on public hearings and focus group data
- Collect information at community centers and other public places
- Confuse "user" data with "community" data
- Use a standardized "off-the-shelf" questionnaire

Benefits

- True local benchmarks established
- Personal biases can be eliminated or discounted
- Credibility to grant agencies and foundations
- Being democratic in decision making
- A small price for very large perception gains and long-term efficient use of funds

About the Author

Ananda Mitra received his PhD from the University of Illinois and is Chair and Professor in the Department of Communication at Wake Forest University. His research includes different forms of data collection methodologies ranging from focus groups to Web-based data collection. He has worked on citizen data collection efforts with nearly a hundred different recreation agencies across the United States.

Index